Travel Publications

CW00871096

LAS VEGAS

must SEES

Chief Editor	Cynthia Clayton Ochterbeck
Senior Editor	M. Linda Lee
Writer	Bobbie Katz
Production Coordinator	Allison M. Simpson
Cartography	Peter Wrenn
Photo Editors	Brigitta L. House, Martha Hunt
Documentation	Doug Rogers; Gayle Sparks Miller
Proofreader	Margo Browning
Production	Octavo Design and Production, Inc. Apopka, Florida
Cover Design	Paris-Venise Design Paris, 17e
Printing and Binding	Quebecor World Laval, Québec

Travel Publications

Michelin North America
One Parkway South
Greenville, SC 29615
USA
800-423-0485
www.michelin-us.com
email: TheGreenGuide@us.michelin.com

Special Sales:

For information regarding bulk sales, customized editions and premium sales, please contact our Customer Service Departments:

USA – 800-423-0485   **Canada** – 800-361-8236

Manufacture française des pneumatiques Michelin
Société en commandite par actions au capital de 304 000 000 EUR
Place des Carmes-Déchaux — 63 Clermont-Ferrand (France)
R.C.S. Clermont-FD B 855 800 507

Note to the reader:

Welcome To Las Vegas

Neptune Bar at Caesars Palace

Table of Contents

The Must Sees

Table of Contents

THE MICHELIN STARS

For more than 75 years, travelers have used the Michelin stars to take the guesswork out of planning a trip. Our star-rating system helps you make the best decision on where to go, what to do, and what to see. A three-star rating means it's one of the "absolutelys"; two stars means it's one of the "should sees"; and one star says it's one of the "sees" —a must if you have the time.

★★★ Absolutely Must See
★★ Really Must See
★ Must See

Three-Star Sights★★★

Bellagio★★★
Death Valley National Park★★★
Grand Canyon National Park★★★
Hoover Dam★★★
Red Rock Country★★★
The Strip★★★
The Venetian★★★

Two-Star Sights★★

Bellagio Fountains★★
Bellagio Gallery of Fine Art★★
Caesars Palace★★
Eiffel Tower★★ at Paris Las Vegas
Forum Shops★★ at Caesars Palace
Fremont Street Experience★★
Grand Canal★★ at The Venetian
Guggenheim Hermitage Museum★★ at The Venetian
Luxor Las Vegas★★
The Mirage★★
New York-New York★★
Paris Las Vegas★★
Red Rock Canyon★★
Red Rock Canyon Natural Conservation Area★★
Sedona★★
Shark Reef★★ at Mandalay Bay

Statue of Liberty★★ at New York-New York
Treasure Island at the Mirage★★
Valley of Fire State Park★★

One-Star Sights★

Aladdin Resort & Casino★
The Auto Collections★ at the Imperial Palace
Bellagio Conservatory and Botanical Gardens★
Bonnie Springs/Old Nevada★
Boulder City★
Brooklyn Bridge★ at New York-New York
CBS Television City★ at MGM Grand
Circus Circus★
Desert Passage★ at the Aladdin
Excalibur★
Folies Bergere★ at the Tropicana Resort & Casino
King Tut's Tomb and Museum★ at Luxor
Lion Habitat★ (MGM Grand)
Lost City Museum of Archaeology★
Madame Tussaud's Celebrity Encounter★
  at The Venetian
Mandalay Bay Resort & Casino★
MGM Grand★
Mirage Volcano★
Mojave National Preserve★
Montezuma Castle National Monument★
Mystère★ (TI)
Nevada State Museum★
"O"★ (Bellagio)
Siegfried & Roy's Secret Garden★ at The Mirage
The Sirens of TI★ at Treasure Island
Spring Mountain Ranch State Park★
Spring Mountains National Recreation Area★
Stratosphere★
Stratosphere Tower★
Tuzigoot National Monument★

LAS VEGAS CALENDAR OF EVENTS

Listed below is a selection of Las Vegas' most
popular annual events. Please note that dates
may change from year to year. For more detailed
information, contact the Las Vegas Convention
and Visitors Authority *(702-892-7573;
www.lasvegas24hrs.com)*.

January
Martin Luther King, Jr. Parade 702-648-8440
Downtown Las Vegas   www.kingweeklasvegas.com

February
Chinese New Year Celebration 702-221-8448
Chinatown Plaza   www.lvchinatown.com
  4255 Spring Mountain Rd.

March
St. Patrick's Celebration 702-678-5777
Fremont St.   www.vegasexperience.com

April
Mardi Gras Festival 702-678-5777
Fremont St.   www.vegasexperience.com

Helldorado Days Rodeo Western Fest 702-895-3900
Thomas and Mack Center   www.thomasandmack.com
  University of Nevada at Las Vegas

Earth Fair 702-455-8200
Sunset Park, 2601 E Sunset Rd.

Annual Invitation Native American Festival 702-455-7955
Clark County Museum   www.co.clark.nv.us
  1830 S. Boulder Hwy.

May
International Food and Folklife Festival 702-455-8200
Clark County   www.accessclarkcounty.com
  Government Center Amphitheater

Cinco de Mayo Festival 702-284-6400
Lorenzi Park, W. Washington St.

June
Jazz Festival 702-678-5777
Fremont St.   www.lasvegasjazzfestival.com

July

Red White and Boom Festival   702-474-4000
Clark County Desert Breeze State Park
    8275 W. Spring Mountain Rd. www.redwhitenboom.com

Summerlin Patriotic Parade   702-341-5500
Hillpointe Rd. & Hills Center Dr.   www.summerlin.com
    Summerlin, NV

September

Shakespeare in the Park   702-384-8427
Henderson Pavilion   www.ci.henderson.nv.us
    200 S. Green Valley Pkwy. Henderson, NV

San Gennaro Street Fair   702-286-4944
Flamingo Rd. & Valley View Blvd. www.sangennarofeast.net

Mexican Independence Day   702-284-6400
Lorenzi Park, W. Washington St.

Greek Food Festival   702-248-3896
St. John's Greek Orthodox Church

Ho'olaule'a Pacific Island Festival   702-382-6939
Lorenzi Park   http://lvhcc.org/hoolaulea
    W. Washington St.

Taste of Vegas   702-243-5922 or 702-455-8200
Clark County   www.tasteofvegas.com
    Government Center Outdoor Amphitheater

Oktoberfest   702-649-8503
German-American Club of America, 1110 E. Lake Mead Blvd.

October

Jaycee State Fair   702-386-7100
Cashman Field, Las Vegas Blvd. N. at Washington St.

Art in the Park   702-294-1611
Bicentennial Park, Boulder City   www.artinthepark.org

Renaissance Festival   702-455-8200
Sunset Park, 2601 E. Sunset Rd.   www.lvrenfair.com

Las Vegas Basque Festival   702-361-6458
Lorenzi Park, W. Washington St.

November

Native American Festival   702-507-3459
Clark County Library

Miss Chinatown Las Vegas   702-221-8448
Chinatown Plaza   www.lvchinatown.com
    4255 Spring Mountain Rd.

December

National Finals Rodeo   888-637-7633
Thomas & Mack Center   www.nfr-rodeo.com
    University of Nevada at Las Vegas

New Year's Eve in Vegas   702-678-5777
Fremont St.   www.las-vegas-new-years-eve.com

Area Code: 702

VISITOR INFORMATION

Before you go, check with the following organizations to obtain the *Las Vegas Official Visitor Guide*, as well as maps and information on accommodations, dining, shopping festivals and recreation:

Las Vegas Visitor Information Center

Operated by the Las Vegas Convention & Visitors Authority
3150 Paradise Road
Las Vegas, NV 89109
702-892-7573; www.lasvegas24hours.com
Open year-round daily 8am–5pm

Las Vegas Chamber of Commerce

3720 Howard Hughes Parkway
Las Vegas, NV 89109
702-735-1616; www.lvchamber.com

> **Try these additional Web sites** for a good idea of what's going on in Vegas:
> www.vegasfreedom.com
> www.lvca.com
> www.lasvegas-nv.com

TIPS FOR SPECIAL VISITORS

Disabled Travelers – Federal law requires that businesses (including hotels and restaurants) provide access for the disabled, devices for the hearing impaired and designated parking spaces. For information, contact the Society for Accessible Travel and Hospitality (SATH), 347 Fifth Ave., Suite 610, New York NY 10016 *(212-447-7284; www.sath.org)*.

All national parks have facilities for the disabled, and offer free or discounted passes *(National Park Service, Office of Public Inquiries, P.O. Box 37127, Room 1013, Washington, DC 20013-7127; 202-208-4747; www.nps.gov)*.

> **In the News**
> Consult the city's major daily newspaper, the *Las Vegas Review Journal* (www.reviewjournal.com), for dining and entertainment news. You'll also learn what's happening in *Nevada Magazine*.

Passengers who will need assistance with train or bus travel should give advance notice to Amtrak *(800-872-7245 or 800-523-6590/TDD; www.amtrak.com)* or Greyhound *(800-752-4841 or 800-345-3109/TDD; www.greyhound.com)*. Make reservations for hand-controlled rental cars in advance with the rental company.

Senior Citizens – Many hotels, attractions and restaurants offer discounts to visitors age 62 or older (proof of age may be required). The **American Association of Retired Persons** (AARP) at 601 E St. NW, Washington DC 20049 *(202-424-3410; www.aarp.com)* offers discounts to its members.

WHEN TO GO

If you can't take the heat, stay out of the oven known as Las Vegas from June until October. With an average of 307 sunny days a year, Las Vegas usually sees only four inches of rain annually (September is the rainiest month). Granted, you won't find the humidity (avg. 29%) here that you do in other parts of the country. Still, Las Vegas sits in the middle of the Mojave Desert and summers can see temperatures in the triple digits, climbing as high as 120°F during the day and only dropping 20 degrees at night. Spring and autumn are milder with temperatures averaging in the 70s. In the winter, temperatures may drop below freezing, although the average high is between 50–60°F.

If you hate crowds, don't come during national holidays, especially when there's a three-day weekend involved. Certain conventions and events also bring in huge numbers of people, sometimes raising room rates sky-high.

Average Seasonal Temperatures in Las Vegas

	Jan	Apr	July	Oct
Avg. High	57°F/14°C	78°F/26°C	104°F/40°C	81°F/27°C
Avg. Low	34°F/1°C	44°F/7°C	68°F/20°C	46°F/8°C

GETTING THERE

By Air – McCarran International Airport, located 4mi southeast of the Strip, handles domestic and international flights *(5757 Wayne Newton Blvd.; 702-261-5743; www.mccarran.com)*. Information desks are located in the baggage-claim area, on the second level above ticketing and in the D Gate area. Shuttles and taxis can be found outside baggage claim *($7; shuttle reservations: 558-9155 or 888-558-9156)*. A taxi ride to the Strip averages $7–$10 to the downtown hotels.

Car rental lots are located off-site; you can catch buses or airport shuttles for a ride to the lots. The Ground Transportation Center near baggage claim has information about shuttles, car rentals and limousine transport.

By Bus – There is no Amtrak train service to Las Vegas, but you can get there by bus. The Greyhound bus station is located downtown *(200 S. Main St.; 800-231-2222; www.greyhound.com)*.

By Car – Direct interstate access to Las Vegas is via I-15, which runs between Butte, Montana, and San Diego, California.

Car Rental Company	Reservations	Internet
Alamo	800-327-9633	www.alamo.com
Avis	800-331-1212	www.avis.com
Budget	800-527-0700	www.drivebudget.com
Dollar	800-800-4000	www.dollar.com
Enterprise	800-325-8007	www.enterprise.com
Hertz	800-654-3131	www.hertz.com
National	800-227-7368	www.nationalcar.com
Thrifty	800-331-4200	www.thrifty.com

GETTING AROUND

By Bus – Buses run from the downtown Transportation Center *(Stewart Ave. & Casino Center Blvd.)* down the Strip past Mandalay Bay and the Four Seasons about every 10 minutes. They stop at designated Citizens Area Transit (CAT) bus stops. Buses to the Strip are $2 one way; pay when you get on *(exact change required)*. Buses off the Strip are $1.25 each way *(exact change required)*. You can obtain timetables for the CAT mass-transit system, which goes all over the city, on buses and in the hotels. The CAT Strip route runs 24hrs a day *(for routes and schedules: 228-7433 or www.rtc.co.clark.nv.us/cat.htm).*

By Taxi – Taxis line up outside the entrance of every hotel. You can't hail a cab from the street; you must go to a designated cab stand or call the cab company.

By Trolley – The Las Vegas Trolley runs to specified hotels every 15 minutes. The red-and-green trolleys operate daily from 9:30am–1:30am, including holidays *($1.50 one way, exact change required; 382-1404).* Trollies serve most of the hotels from Mandalay Bay to the Stratosphere.

By Monorail – Monorails *(free of charge)* run between many hotel properties: MGM Grand–Bally's; Bellagio–Monte Carlo; Mirage–Treasure Island; and Mandalay Bay–Excalibur–Luxor. In 2004 a monorail is scheduled to begin operating from the airport to most of the hotels on the Strip, all the way to Fremont Street downtown.

Walking The Strip – The Las Vegas Strip (Las Vegas Blvd.) is 3.5mi long, running from Russell Road (by Mandalay Bay) to Charleston Boulevard, and then on to downtown. To get your bearings, you need to know that the Strip is crossed by five major streets—Russell, Tropicana, Flamingo, Spring Mountain and Sahara.

Overhead walkways connect several Strip properties: New York-New York, the MGM Grand, the Tropicana and Excalibur over the junction of Las Vegas Boulevard and Tropicana Avenue; and Caesars Palace, Bellagio and Bally's over the junction of Las Vegas Boulevard and Flamingo Road.

By Car – Don't drive unless you know the back entrances to the hotels and can avoid the Strip, which tends to be gridlocked at all hours of the day. All the Strip hotels have valet parking *(standard tip for valet attendants is $1).* The speed limit on the Strip is 35mph; seat belts must be worn at all times.

Important Phone Numbers		
Emergency (24hrs)		911
Police (non-emergency)		311
Medical Services, House Calls USA		800-468-3537
Dental Services, Clark County Dental Society		732-5373
24hr Pharmacies		
Walgreens	1101 Las Vegas Blvd. S.	471-6844
Sav-On	3250 Las Vegas Blvd.	643-8538
Poison Control		800-446-6179
Time/Weather		248-4800

FOREIGN VISITORS

In addition to the tourism offices throughout Nevada, visitors from outside the US can obtain information from the Web site of the Las Vegas Convention and Visitors Authority *(www.lasvegas24hrs.com),* or from the US embassy or consulate in their country of residence. For a complete list of American consulates and embassies abroad, visit the Web site for the Department of State Bureau of Consular Affairs *(http://travel.state.gov/links.html).*

Entry Requirements – Starting October 1, 2003, travelers entering the United States under the Visa Waiver Program (VWP) must have a machine-readable passport. Any traveler without a machine-readable passport will be required to obtain a visa before entering the US. Citizens of VWP countries are permitted to enter the US for general business or tourist purposes for a maximum of 90 days without needing a visa. Requirements for the Visa Waiver Program can be found at the Department of State's Visa Services Web site *(http://travel.state.gov/vwp.html)*.

All citizens of nonparticipating countries must have a visitor's visa. Upon entry, nonresident foreign visitors must present a valid passport and round-trip transportation ticket. Canadian citizens are not required to present a passport or visa, but they must present a valid picture ID and proof of citizenship. Naturalized Canadian citizens should carry their citizenship papers.

US Customs – All articles brought into the US must be declared at the time of entry. Prohibited items: plant material; firearms and ammunition (if not for sporting purposes); meat or poultry products. For information, contact the US Customs Service, 1300 Pennsylvania Ave. NW, Washington, DC 20229 *(202-927-6724; www.customs.gov/travel/travel.htm)*.

Money and Currency Exchange – Visitors can exchange currency at downtown banks as well as at McCarran International Airport. For cash transfers, Western Union *(800-325-6000; www.westernunion.com)* has agents throughout the US. Banks, stores, restaurants and hotels accept travelers' checks with picture identification. To report a lost or stolen credit card: American Express *(800-528-4800)*; Diners Club *(800-234-6377)*; MasterCard *(800-307-7309)*; or Visa *(800-336-8472)*.

Driving in the US – Visitors bearing valid driver's licenses issued by their country of residence are not required to obtain an International Driver's License. Drivers must carry vehicle registration and/or rental contract, and proof of automobile insurance at all times. Gasoline is sold by the gallon. Vehicles in the US are driven on the right-hand side of the road.

Electricity – Voltage in the US is 120 volts AC, 60 Hz. Foreign-made appliances may need AC adapters (available at specialty travel and electronics stores) and North American flat-blade plugs.

Taxes and Tipping – Prices displayed in the US do not include sales tax (7.25% in Nevada), which is not reimbursable. It is customary to give a small gift of money—a tip—for services rendered, to waiters (15–20% of bill), porters ($1 per bag), chamber maids ($1 per day) and cab drivers (15% of fare).

Measurement Equivalents

Degrees Fahrenheit	95°	86°	77°	68°	59°	50°	41°	32°	23°	14°
Degrees Celsius	35°	30°	25°	20°	15°	10°	5°	0°	-5°	-10°

1 inch = 2.54 centimeters   1 foot = 30.48 centimeters

1 mile = 1.609 kilometers   1 pound = 0.454 kilograms

1 quart = 0.946 liters   1 gallon = 3.785 liters

Must Know: Practical Information

ACCOMMODATIONS
For a list of suggested accommodations, see Must Stay.

For the best deal, book your room in advance. Room rates are dependent on occupancy; the higher the occupancy at a property, the more the rooms will cost. For that reason, prices fluctuate from day to day (sometimes even within the same day). At certain times of the year, it's possible to get a luxury hotel room or suite at a budget price or you might end up paying top prices for a low-rent room. As a rule of thumb, prices are lower during the week and in low-occupancy months (traditionally during the summer and in January). Rates are highest on the Strip, but the convenience of being near the action is worth the extra cost. Rooms downtown, and especially off the Strip, will be quieter and less expensive.

Las Vegas Convention and Visitors Authority reservation service: *800-332-5333.*

Major hotel and motel chains with locations in Las Vegas include:

Property	Phone/Web site	Property	Phone/Web site
Best Western	800-528-1234 www.bestwestern.com	Hyatt	800-233-1234 www.hyatt.com
Comfort, Clarion & Quality Inns	800-228-5150 www.comfortinn.com	ITT Sheraton	800-325-3535 www.sheraton.com
Crowne Plaza	800-227-6963 www.crowneplaza.com	Marriott	800-228-9290 www.marriott.com
Days Inn	800-325-2525 www.daysinn.com	Ramada	800-228-2828 www.ramada.com
Hilton	800-445-8667 www.hilton.com	Ritz-Carlton	800-241-3333 www.ritzcarlton.com
Holiday Inn	800-465-4329 www.holiday-inn.com	Westin	800-848-0016 www.westin.com
Howard Johnson	800-446-4656 www.hojo.com		

Campgrounds are available in Mt. Charleston, Dolomite Campgrounds and Kyle Canyon Campgrounds; all are run by the US Forest Service *(873-8800; www.fs.fed.us).* There is also camping in Red Rock Canyon *(363-1921; www.redrockcanyon.blm.gov).*

RV Parks in Las Vegas have full hook-ups and accept pets. Rates generally run less than $20 a night. Reservations are recommended.

California RV Park	*Stewart Ave. at Main St.*	*388-2602 or 800-634-6505.*
Circusland RV Park	*500 Circus Circus Dr.*	*794-3757 or 800-634-3450.*
KOA Campground	*4315 Boulder Hwy.*	*451-5527 or 800-562-7782.*
Silverton Hotel Casino and RV Park	*3333 Blue Diamond Rd.*	*263-7777 or 800-588-7711.*

SPORTS AND RECREATION
For information about gambling, see p 31.

Yes, there is life after gaming and much of it is outdoors. From golf, tennis and cycling to boating at Lake Mead, rock climbing at Red Rock Canyon, or skiing on Mt. Charleston, there's no lack of things to do. Unfortunately for spectator-sports fans, there are no national league baseball or football teams in Las Vegas.

Car Racing – A 1,500-acre motorsports complex, Las Vegas Motor Speedway *(7000 Las Vegas Blvd. North; 644-4444; www.lvms.com)* can accommodate up to 107,000 spectators. Drag races, NASCAR events, short-track races, motocross and a variety of other contests are held here. Highlights include the annual Las Vegas 400, a Winston Cup event held in March, and the Indy Racing League's open-wheel Las Vegas 500 in April.

The Ranch Experience	
If you have a hankering for the Old West, some cattle roping, camping out, or riding off into the sunset (often with a campfire dinner), here are some places to contact:	
Sandy Valley Ranch	631-0463
Sagebrush Ranch	645-9422
Red Rock Ranch	387-2457
Mt. Charleston Riding Stables	387-2457
Bonnie Springs Ranch	875-4191
Spring Mountain Ranch	798-7788

College Sports – Fans can watch the University of Las Vegas Runnin' Rebels play football and basketball *(campus bordered by Maryland Pkwy., Tropicana Ave., Paradise Rd & Flamingo Rd.)*. Basketball games are held at the Thomas & Mack Center *(4505 Maryland Pkwy.)*. Catch football matches at Sam Boyd Stadium *(7000 Russell Rd.)*. For tickets: 702-739-3267 or www.unlvtickets.com.

Golf – Las Vegas currently boasts more than 50 major golf courses, designed by such big-name players as Arnold Palmer, Robert Trent Jones Sr., Pete Dye and Billy Casper. Most of the hotels have access to courses; the concierge can set up tee times for you. A few hotels (Caesars Palace, Rio, MGM Grand) even have their own offsite golf courses.

Two public courses (considered the two toughest in Vegas) offer seasonal rates: Badlands *(242-4653)* and Wildhorse *(434-9000)*.

Request a copy of *Golfing Las Vegas*, published by *VegasGolfer* magazine, from the Las Vegas Golf/Visitor Information *(800-762-0296; www.lasvegasgolf.com)*.

Boxing – Las Vegas has become a boxing mecca with championship fights held at the MGM Grand, Mandalay Bay and Caesars Palace. Ringside seats can cost as much as $1,500 while the "cheap" seats go for $100–$200.

Rodeo – Every year, the National Finals Rodeo (NFR) and the Professional Bull Riders World Finals *(November)* are held in Las Vegas. In December, the NFR brings in hordes of people along with the Cowboy Christmas Show, held at the Las Vegas Convention Center. Admission is

It's Showtime!
At Vegas casinos, showtimes, prices and dark days (when the show isn't held) will often change, so call the hotel box office to get the most up-to-date information.

free and the merchandise is terrific (if you like turquoise jewelry and western garb). The NFR is held at the Thomas & Mack Center *(on the University of Las Vegas campus, 4505 Maryland Pkwy.; 895-3900; www.nfr-rodeo.com)*.

Las Vegas

The Neon Jungle: Las Vegas

Planet Vegas? The idea is not so far out as you might think for a place that possesses its own unique atmosphere, sizzling heat, and neon-brightness factor. Not to mention its three Gs—glitz, glitter and glamour—created more than a half-century ago. Vegas added another G in recent years, the gee-whiz factor, which came into play at the dawning of the megaresort era in the 1990s.

Set in Las Vegas Valley, surrounded by mountain ranges and beyond by the forbidding sands of the Mojave Desert, Las Vegas has gone from being a quiet spot in the desert to a world-class resort destination. The history of the city's blooming is quite a colorful one. Twelve thousand years ago or so, Las Vegas was a marsh covered with lush vegetation. As eon after eon passed, the marsh receded and the rivers disappeared. What remained was an arid, parched landscape that could nurture only the hardiest of plants and animals.

Water trapped underground in the geological strata of the Las Vegas Valley sporadically surfaced to nourish the plants, creating an oasis in the desert as the life-giving water flowed to the Colorado River. Protected from discovery by the harsh desert that surrounded it, the site that would become Las Vegas was hidden for centuries from all but the Native Americans.

Then on Christmas Day in 1829, a Mexican trader named Antonio Armijo was leading a 60-man party along the Spanish Trail to Los Angeles when he veered from the usual route. While his caravan was resting about 100mi northeast of present-day Vegas, a scouting party rode west in search of water. Raphael Rivera, an experienced 18-year-old Mexican scout, ventured into the Las Vegas desert. It was there he discovered Las Vegas Springs. Sometime between 1830 and 1848, the name "Vegas," as shown on maps of that day, was changed to Las Vegas, Spanish for "the meadows."

The Mormons were the first group to settle in the area. In 1855 members of the Church of Latter-Day Saints built a fort out of sun-dried adobe bricks near Las Vegas Creek *(see Historic Sites)*. But it was the advent of the railroad that

led to the founding of Las Vegas on May 15, 1905. That was the day that the Union Pacific auctioned off 1,200 lots in a single day in an area that is now the Fremont Street Experience, a traffic-free, mall-like setting.

Nevada became the first state to legalize casino-style gambling and was also, very reluctantly, the last western state to outlaw it during Prohibition in the first decade of the 20C. At midnight on October 1, 1910, a strict anti-gambling law took effect in Nevada. This law even prohibited the Western custom of flipping a coin for the price of a drink.

For many years after gambling was legalized in 1931, the Mafia ruled Las Vegas. During the early years of the Strip, it was no holds barred—with "no" being the operative word. There was no cover charge, no minimum charge, no state speed limit, no sales tax, no waiting period for marriages, no state income tax, and no regulation of gambling as there is today.

Cashing In On Casinos

Thanks to gamblers who hastily set up illegal underground games, gambling flourished despite Prohibition. Finally, in 1931 the Nevada legislature legalized gambling. The first hotel to go up was the El Rancho Vegas, which triggered a building boom in the late 1940s. By far the most celebrated of the early resorts was the Flamingo Hotel, a classy "carpet joint" modeled on the fancy resort hotels in Miami and built by Benjamin "Bugsy" Siegel, a member of the Meyer Lansky crime organization. With its giant pink neon sign and replicas of pink flamingos on the lawn, the Flamingo opened on New Year's Eve, 1946. Six months later, Siegel was murdered by an unknown gunman.

It wasn't until after 1966, when billionaire Howard Hughes arrived in the city to live at the Desert Inn (which he purchased), that a law passed by the Nevada legislature allowed publicly traded corporations to obtain gambling licenses. Gradually, legally obtained capital started to flow into the city. In the 21C, the financial foundations of Las Vegas are firmly anchored in legitimate corporations, which spare no expense trying to outdo each other by building one fabulous megaresort after another.

Vegas just wouldn't be Vegas without its casinos. The gaming houses that once lit Las Vegas Boulevard with flashing neon have now mushroomed into spectacular themed megaresorts incorporating hotels, restaurants, art museums, animal habitats, and pretty much anything else you can imagine— and some things you can't! Here you'll find reproductions of the Eiffel Tower in Paris, Venice's Grand Canal, and the Sphinx in Egypt. Ogle all you want. If there was ever an eye-popping experience, Vegas is it!

For a legend of price listings for hotels, see Must Stays.

Bellagio★★★

3600 Las Vegas Blvd. S.
702-693-7111 or
888-987-7111.
www.bellagiolasvegas.com.
3,005 rooms. **$$$$$**.

Fine art, gardens, fashion. These are hardly things that you used to associate with a casino in Las Vegas. But that was before this hotel's vision changed the landscape of the gambling mecca. When Steve Wynn opened the $1.7-billion Bellagio in October 1998 (it's now owned by MGM Mirage), he created a place of ideal beauty and comfort. Considered one of the most opulent

The Strip★★★
The city's greatest concentration of resorts and casinos lies along a 4.5mi stretch of Las Vegas Boulevard known as the Strip. Beginning at the Stratosphere and reaching south to Mandalay Bay Resort *2000–4000 blocks of Las Vegas Blvd.)*, the Strip is a carnival of sensational architecture and streetside displays.

upscale resorts in the world, this 36-story property was inspired by the village of Bellagio on the shores of Lake Como in northern Italy.

An eight-acre lake, the scene of spectacular **fountain and light shows★★**, graces the front of the complex. Inside, the hotel's casino is arguably the most posh in town; try your hand at a game of Texas Hold 'em or 7-Card Stud in the smoke-free Poker Room.

Art For Your Sake
- Exhibits in the **Bellagio Gallery of Fine Art★★** *(see Museums)*, the Strip's first art museum, change about every six months.
- The striking multicolored **glass ceiling** in the lobby is an installation by famed Washington glass artist Dale Chihuly.
- Off the lobby is the **Bellagio Conservatory** and **Botanical Gardens★** *(see Free Vegas)*, with seasonally changing gardens and special holiday displays.

The Venetian★★★

3355 Las Vegas Blvd. S.
702-414-4405 or 888-283-6423.
www.venetian.com.
4,047 suites. $$$$$.

Never been to Venice? Don't despair! **St. Mark's Square**, the **Doge's Palace**, the **Campanile** and the **Grand Canal**★★ are closer than you think—at the Venetian in Las Vegas. The world's largest all-suite hotel and convention complex, the Venetian boosted its suite count to a staggering 4,047 units in June 2003. Designed to painstakingly reproduce the city of Venice, the hotel is located on the site where the venerable Sands Hotel Casino—a Las Vegas institution and the home of the famed Rat Pack—stood from 1952 until it was imploded in 1996. The casino is decked out with reproductions of famous frescoes on the ceiling and marble on the floor. More than 122 table games include a semi-private area for high-stakes Baccarat.

First phase of a planned 6,000-suite resort, the $1.2-billion property opened in May 1999. At the Venetian you can update your wardrobe at the Grand Canal Shoppes *(see Must Shop)*, which house 75 of the world's most exclusive retailers, or take a gondola ride—complete with serenade—through the canal that winds around the shops and restaurants. From the Strip you can access Sephora, a 13,000sq ft store filled to the brim with cosmetics and hair- and skin-care products. And be sure to save up for a dinner at Wolfgang Puck's acclaimed Postrio restaurant.

What Else Is There To Do?

- Enjoy Michael Flatley's Lord of the Dance and a variety show called "V" in the hotel's 1,400-seat **Venetian showroom.**
- Wax philosophical at **Madame Tussaud's Celebrity Encounter**★, where the statues are so lifelike that sometimes it's hard to tell the inanimate from the animate *(see Museums).*
- Luxuriate at **Canyon Ranch Spa's** freestanding 63,000sq ft health spa and fitness club *(see Must be Pampered).*
- Admire fine art at the world-renowned **Guggenheim Hermitage Museum**★★, where exhibits change approximately twice a year.

Caesars Palace★★

3570 Las Vegas Blvd. S.
702-731-7110 or 800-634-6661.
www.parkplace.com/caesars.
2,427 rooms. **$$$$.**

Even Julius would have been proud of this majestic hotel that can rightfully claim to be the first theme resort in Las Vegas. Caesars Palace, which opened in 1966, cost $25 million to build (they've added more than $1 billion in renovations since) and stretches over 85 acres.

The Greco-Roman extravaganza (with statues to match) encompasses spectacular fountains, three casinos, 21 restaurants, a health spa, a beauty salon, the Appian Way shopping area, tennis courts and 4 entertainment lounges. Within its 29,000sq ft of luxe casino space, Caesars offers slot machines that accept amounts from 5¢ to $500.

In 1998 Caesars added a 4.5-acre Garden of the Gods outdoor area with three swimming pools. In 2003 the property experienced a renaissance when a new 4,100-seat Coliseum showroom opened, boasting Celine Dion as its headliner, and the hotel's latest oh-so-upscale restaurant, Bradley Ogden, joined the ranks of Spago and The Palm.

Chariot of the Goods

- Caesars is the gateway to the $100-million **Forum Shops**★★, a chi-chi mall covered by a domed ceiling that changes from day to night *(see Must Shop)*. You'll think you're walking down the streets of Rome when you wander the Forum Shops, amid columns, piazzas and statuary.
- Take a ride to the good life via a central people-mover that transports you from the Strip into the hotel. The hotel's rotunda houses a miniature city of Rome, as it may have appeared 2,000 years ago.
- If you want to take a ride, try the **Race For Atlantis** virtual-reality attraction in the Forum Shops.

Luxor Las Vegas★★

3900 Las Vegas Blvd. S. 702-262-4000 or 800-288-1000. www.luxor.com. 4,692 rooms. **$$$**.

Walk like an Egyptian through this 30-story **pyramid**, with a 29-million-cubic-foot atrium at its apex. Fabulous reproductions of artifacts from Luxor, Egypt as well as the Karnak Temple line the walls of the hotel, along with copies of hieroglyphics found in the Egypt's Valley of the Kings. You'll enter the hotel beneath a massive 10-story replica of the **Sphinx**. From there, you'll be transported to your room by "inclinator," an elevator that travels up the interior slope of the 350ft pyramid at a 39-degree angle.

The hotel was named after Luxor, a city in Egypt that was built in the New Kingdom between 1550 BC and 1070 BC. Opened in 1993, the hotel cost $375 million to build. Its opulent round casino includes a lavish poker room and a race and sports book with 17 giant-screen TVs. Three years after it opened, the property debuted its twin towers as part of a $400-million expansion, and added the first IMAX 3D theater in Las Vegas.

Midnight Fantasy

At the Luxor's Pharaoh Theater. 800-288-1000. www.luxor.com. Guests must be at least 21.

When the clock strikes midnight at the Luxor, sit back and enjoy this adult revue—a series of 14 vignettes choreographed to popular music and performed by sexy dancers. From the Egyptian-themed opening to the high-energy hip-hop number, the provocative choreography is guaranteed to grab your attention.

Keys to the Kingdom

- **King Tut's Tomb and Museum**★ contains authentic replicas of items found in King Tutankhamen's tomb and is the only full-scale reproduction outside of Egypt *(see Museums)*.
- The IMAX Ridefilm, **In Search of the Obelisk** provides high-impact simulated thrills *(see Thrill Rides)*.
- By night, a 315,000-watt laser beam—the **Xenon Light**★★—shoots out from the top of the pyramid; it's visible as far as 250mi away in Los Angeles.

MGM Grand★★

3799 Las Vegas Blvd. S.
702-891-1111 or 800-646-7787.
www.mgmgrand.com.
5,034 rooms. **$$$$$**.

Currently considered the largest hotel in the world, this 114-acre city within a city really roars with amenities: gourmet and specialty restaurants; a 6.6-acre pool and spa complex; Studio 54 nightclub; the 17,157-seat MGM Grand Garden for superstar concerts and world-championship sporting events, Studio Walk shopping, and **CBS Television City**★, featuring a studio walk with screening rooms for TV pilots.

The Hollywood-themed MGM Grand, which premiered in December 1993 at a cost of $1 billion, boasts a mind-boggling 5,000-plus rooms in its 30-story towers. Six years after it opened, the hotel underwent a $575-million expansion, adding two wedding chapels, a 9,000sq ft lion habitat, and the Mansions, a high-roller complex comprising 29 private villas (ranging in size from 2,400–12,000sq ft).

Lions and Lions and Lions . . . Oh My!

In MGM Grand's casino, gaming takes on a whole new meaning. Besides 3,500 slot machines and 165 table games, the hotel has real MGM lions right in the middle of the casino. Kids from 8 to 80 will enjoy the **Lion Habitat**★, located near Studio 54 in the middle of the gaming area. Lions romp through the three-story naturalistic structure and walk right over your head (thanks to the wonders of bullet-proof safety glass) in full view. When there are cubs, you can even have a picture taken with them!

That's Entertainment

The hotel has two main showrooms:

- The theater that was the longtime home of the city's first special-effects spectacle, EFX, closed in December 2002 to make way for a new Cirque du Soleil production. The totally renovated theater and its new show will debut in 2004.

- The 700-seat Hollywood Theatre presents star headliners like Tom Jones, Paul Anka and David Copperfield, 365 days a year.

The Mirage★★

3400 Las Vegas Blvd. S.
702-791-7111 or
800-627-6667.
www.themirage.com.
3,050 rooms. **$$$$$**.

You'll think you're seeing things when you check in at the Mirage—in front of a 20,000-gallon aquarium full of colorful fish (and a few sharks). A few steps into the hotel, you'll encounter a Polynesian fantasy of lush gardens under a 90ft-high glass-enclosed atrium filled with royal palms and tropical foliage. The rain forest theme extends into the casino, where the blackjack tables have the best rules in town. Outside, there's a lagoon with waterfalls and a giant **volcano**★ that erupts every 15 minutes after dark.

If this sounds like a tropical paradise, that's what it's supposed to be. This resort, which opened in November 1989 to the tune of $630 million, is credited with being the property that triggered the boom of themed mega-resorts up and down the Las Vegas Strip in the early to mid-1990s. Here you can see exotic wildlife up close and personal, thanks to Siegfried & Roy, or enjoy a close encounter of the celebrity kind at the show starring impersonator Danny Gans.

Where The Animals Play

The Mirage is home to **The Secret Garden of Siegfried & Roy**★, a lush sanctuary for six rare breeds of exotic cats (and one 55-year-old four-ton elephant) including the duo's rare white tigers that star in their show. The habitat provides a way for Siegfried & Roy, conservationists who have established breeding programs on three continents to save the white tiger and white lion from extinction, to share the results of their efforts with the public.

Adjoining the Secret Garden is the **Dolphin Habitat**, a breeding and research facility for Atlantic bottlenose dolphins.

Casinos

New York-New York★★

3790 Las Vegas Blvd. S. 702-740-6969 or 800-693-6763. www.nynyhotelcasino.com. 2,024 rooms. **$$$$$**.

Start spreading the news: this stellar resort—the tallest casino in Nevada at 47 stories (529ft)—depicts the familiar New York skyline with re-creations of familiar landmarks. A replica of the **Statue of Liberty★★** is the resort's signature; it's surrounded by 12 New York City towers, including a re-creation of the **Empire State Building** (47 stories), the Century Building (41 stories) and the Chrysler Building (40 stories). There's even a 300ft-long model of the **Brooklyn Bridge★**. The **Manhattan Express**, a Coney Island-style roller coaster, travels around the skyscrapers at speeds up to 60 miles per hour. Inside, you'll walk by familiar New York sites such as Park Avenue, Central Park, and Times Square around the crowded 84,000sq ft casino with its flashing neon lights.

New York-New York is a great place to experience great apple martinis; a Coney Island arcade; a bar with dueling pianists; an authentic Irish pub; Cirque du Soleil's newest production, Zumanity (called the company's creative climax to sensuality, humanity and art); and the hilarious comedy of Rita Rudner.

New York-New York for Sports Fans & Bar Flies

ESPN Zone – A premier sports and dining complex made up of three individual, yet integrated, components. The first is the Studio Grill, where you can enjoy generous portions of American fare. Then there's the Screening Room, featuring two 14-inch screens surrounded by a dozen 36-inch monitors for broadcasting live sports events. Last, but not least, the Sports Arena boasts 10,000sq ft of interactive and competitive games.

Coyote Ugly – This southern-style bar and dance saloon is patterned after the original Coyote Ugly bar in New York City, the one that inspired the blockbuster movie produced by Jerry Bruckheimer. Each night, sexy bartenders climb atop the bar to perform a bold show filled with stunts ranging from fire-blowing to body shots, clogging and choreographed dance numbers—and the best part is, you can join in the fun!

Paris Las Vegas★★

3655 Las Vegas Blvd. S.
702-946-7000 or 888-266-5687.
www.parislv.com.
2,916 rooms. **$$$**.

Ooh-la-la! If you want to experience the City of Lights and can't afford the airfare, give this hotel a go. Although its namesake city lies across the ocean, Paris Las Vegas strives to capture the essence of Paris, France. Here you can dine 100ft above the Strip in a 50-story replica of the **Eiffel Tower★★**, or whiz up in a glass elevator to an observation deck overlooking the Las Vegas Valley (not to be confused with the Left Bank).

The place even looks like Paris, with a reproduction of the **Arc de Triomphe**, and facades of **L'Opera**, the Louvre and the Hôtel de Ville. Owned by Park Place Entertainment, this resort opened in September 1999 with Catherine Deneuve, Charles Aznavour and Michel LeGrand in attendance. It cost a cool $790 million to build and its authenticity extends from the French phrases spoken by the employees, to the security guards clad in gendarme uniforms. Three legs of the Eiffel Tower rest on the floor of the casino, whose Parisian streetscapes provide the oh-so-chic setting for 90 table games and more than 1,700 slot machines.

Champagne, Sparkling Wine, Cigars?
A must-not-miss on Le Boulevard at Paris Las Vegas is **Napoleon's Champagne Bar**, which offers a selection of more than 100 champagnes and sparkling wines by the bottle and by the glass, complemented by a light menu of hors d'oeuvres. For smokers, Napoleon's features a cigar bar with a walk-in humidor. Live entertainment nightly makes this a popular nightspot.

Paris is connected to its sister property, Bally's, by Le Boulevard, a Parisian-style shopping district, complete with cobblestone streets, street lamps and authentic French boutiques and eateries. If you're a pastry lover, don't miss Lenôtre and the Boulangerie, which bakes its own fresh breads. The property also boasts one of the city's best (and most expensive) buffets, a showroom, and a wonderful spa.

Treasure Island at the Mirage★★

3300 Las Vegas Blvd. S. at Spring Mountain Rd. 702-894-7111 or 800-288-7206. www.treasureislandlas vegas.com. 2,900 rooms. **$$$.**

When you walk across the draw-bridge that spans the man-made bay in front of this hotel, you'll step into the world of Robert Louis Stevenson's adventure novel *Treasure Island*. Outside, waves lap at a replica of a small island village. Inside, overflowing treasure chests line the walls, and the carpets are patterned with jewels and gold doubloons. The huge casino has friendly dealers and non-intimidating table games for beginners; Players Club members earn double points on selected slot machines.

Ho Ho Ho and a Bottle of Rum

The trendy new nightspot at Treasure Island is **Mist**, which showcases high-tech entertainment. Here you can relax and watch your favorite music videos or sports games on one of the oversized plasma-screen TVs while the wait staff caters to your almost-every whim.

Site of the famed **The Pirate Battle of Buccaneer Bay★★** on the Strip, Treasure Island is currently in the process of revamping its signature show—and the venue's image along with it—for the hotel's 10th anniversary in October 2003. In anticipation of the hipper image that's emerging, the property now refers to itself simply as "TI."

The Sirens of TI★, the new pirate battle attraction unveiled in October 2003, is a more contemporary version of the original show, incorporating sexy sirens into the plot. If you can't find a place on the sidewalk to watch the fun, grab a table at the hotel's Buccaneer Bay restaurant, whose windows overlook the "bay." (Of course, you have to eat there to watch, but the food won't disappoint.)

Aladdin Resort & Casino★

3667 Las Vegas Blvd. South. 702-785-5555 or 877-333-WISH. www.aladdincasino.com. 2,500 rooms. **$$$.**

You'll enjoy many wonderful Arabian nights in this Moroccan-style resort that arose in the place of the original Aladdin, imploded in 1998. This $3.1-billion hotel houses **The London Club**, a European-style gaming salon, as well as dining, entertainment, a spa, and a casino with a *1001 Arabian Nights* theme. The 7,000-seat Theatre for the Performing Arts hosts big-name concerts and an annual Broadway show series. **The Desert Passage★**, a retail and dining complex, connects to the hotel *(see Must Shop)*.

Circus Circus★

2880 Las Vegas Blvd. S. 702-734-0410 or 800-634-3450. www.circuscircus.com. 4,000 rooms. **$$-$$$**.

Opened in 1968, Circus Circus was the city's first gaming establishment to offer entertainment for all ages. Initially there was a casino and a carnival midway, but no hotel rooms. The first 400 rooms were built in 1972. Today the casino occupies the main floor, while the second floor is a fantasyland of carnival games, state-of-the-art arcade games and a circus arena. The **Adventuredome** indoor theme park was added in 1993.

Excalibur★

3850 Las Vegas Blvd. S. 702-597-7777 or 800-937-7777. www.excalibur-casino.com. 4,008 rooms. **$$$**.

Ever dream of traveling back in time to an age of jousting knights? Enter the world of King Arthur (a great place to bring the kids) via this sparkling medieval castle. In **King Arthur's Arena**, you can eat with your hands and cheer the action during the Tournament of Kings. Keeping with the Camelot theme, the hotel's shopping mall is a medieval village. There's also a male dance revue that would likely make King Arthur blush.

Mandalay Bay Resort & Casino★

3950 Las Vegas Blvd. S. 702-632-7777 or 877-632-7000. www.mandalaybay.com. 3,660 rooms. **$$$**.

Life is a beach at Mandalay Bay. This tropical-themed resort possesses the only sand-and-surf beach on the Strip. Besides its casino, the property boasts an 11-acre **lagoon**, a three-quarter-mile lazy river ride, 15 restaurants, night-clubs, shops, the hit show MAMMA MIA!, and **Shark Reef**★★ aquarium *(see Fishy Vegas)*, and the renowned House of Blues (don't miss their Sunday Gospel Brunch). And you can take the monorail from Mandalay Bay to its sister properties, Luxor and Excalibur.

Stratosphere★

2000 Las Vegas Blvd. S. 702-380-7777 or 800-998-6937. www.stratlv.com. 2,444 rooms. **$$-$$$**.

This property is the height of Vegas spectacular—its **tower**★ is the tallest freestanding structure west of the Mississippi. Thanks to the world's highest thrill rides, **High Roller** and **Big Shot** *(see Must Ride)* a wonderful revolving restaurant, and two **observation decks** with great **views**★★★, you can literally keep your nose in the air for hours. Stratosphere's productions include American Superstars and Viva Las Vegas, the city's longest-running afternoon show.

Casinos

Flamingo Las Vegas

3555 Las Vegas Blvd. S.
702-733-3111 or 800-732-2111.
www.flamingolasvegas.com.
3,642 rooms. **$$-$$$**.

The name Flamingo Hotel has
survived from the 1940's era of
Strip development, but in 1993
the Hilton Corporation razed
the Flamingo's original motel-
style buildings, including the
fortress-like "Bugsy's Suite"
(named after the hotel's creator,
Bugsy Siegel) with its false
stairways and bulletproof office.
Today the Flamingo comprises
six towers filled with guest
rooms, multiple swimming
pools, a wedding chapel in a
tropical setting, and a wildlife
habitat. Gladys Knight, The
Amazing Johnathan and The
Second City comedy troupe
perform here.

Imperial Palace Hotel & Casino

3535 Las Vegas Blvd. S. 702-731-3311 or 800-634-6441. www.imperialpalace.com.
2,700 rooms. **$$-$$$**.

There is more to this pagoda-roofed casino hotel than meets the eye. Although its casino is no match for the grandeur of the megaresorts, inside the
hotel is a widespread complex with restaurants, an Olympic-size pool, a spa, a
showroom where "Legends in Concert" appears, and **The Auto Collections**★
of antique cars *(see Museums)*. During the summer, the Imperial Palace hosts
its celebrated Hawaiian luaus by the pool.

Tropicana Resort & Casino

3801 Las Vegas Blvd. S. 702-739-2222 or 800-634-4000. www.tropicanalv.com.
1,800 rooms. **$$-$$$**.

In recent years, this Polynesian-themed hotel has undergone renovations that
include the creation of a shopping arcade and new restaurants. Splash around
in the water park, equipped with three pools (featuring swim-up blackjack in
summer), a waterslide, five spas, two lagoons, tropical plants and live flamingos. Noted for the 4,000sq ft **stained-glass ceiling** that curves over the
main casino floor, The Tropicana also hosts the **Folies Bergere**★, Las Vegas'
longest-running production show. Guests staying at the Tropicana during the
summer months can play swim-up blackjack in the property's 12,000sq ft pool.

GAMBLING

Oh, the games people play—blackjack, craps, keno, roulette, slot machines, video poker and more. Where Las Vegas is concerned, it's all in the game. Gambling made the city what it is, and gambling remains its tour de force. Here are a few of the games of chance that gambling brings to the table:

Blackjack – The object is to draw cards that add up to 21 or as close to 21 as possible without going over that magic number. Everybody at the table bets against the dealer. If the dealer's first two cards total 16 or under, the dealer must "hit," or draw additional cards. If they add up to 17 or over, the dealer must stand. If the player's cards add up to more than the dealer's, but are under 21, the player wins. If the situation is reversed, the house wins (or they can tie and nobody wins). An ace and a picture card together constitute Blackjack, which automatically wins.

Craps – On the first or "come out" roll in this fast-paced dice game, the "shooter" throws the dice to the other end of the table (dice must hit the wall of the table to be considered a legal roll). The shooter tries to establish a number—four, five, six, eight, nine or ten—then he tries to roll that number again before he rolls a seven.

Tip Your Dealer
If you want to slip the dealer a couple of bucks, make sure you do it in between hands, or spins. Or you can wait until the session's over. It wouldn't hurt to tip the people that bring you change, too—especially if you hit the jackpot.

Roulette – The roulette table is covered with 36 numbers plus a green zero and a green double zero (the European layout has only one zero). Half of the 36 numbers are red and half are black. Players may place chips on any combination of numbers. The winner is determined by where the marble-like ball comes to rest when the croupier spins the wheel.

Historic Sites

There are many different stages of Las Vegas' Old West history—a couple will even ride you clear out of town to places like Boulder City and Overton. From the days of cowboys and Indians to the building of Hoover Dam to magnates like Howard Hughes, Vegas' colorful past comes alive at these sites.

Bonnie Springs/Old Nevada★

1 Gunfighter Lane, Blue Diamond, NV. From the Strip, take Charleston Blvd. west for 25mi. 702-875-4191. www.bonniesprings.com. Shuttles are available from the Strip (call Star Land Tours, 702-296-4972). Open daily May–Sept 10:30am–6pm, Oct–Apr 10:30am–5pm. $7/car weekdays, $10 weekends.

Riding The Range

The ranch offers the perfect base from which to explore Red Rock Canyon on horseback. Horses can be rented through the Red Rock Riding Stables on the property. Or you can take the guided two-hour sunset trail ride through the canyons, which culminates in a breathtaking sunset followed by a campfire dinner—steak, salad, baked potato, corn on the cob.

If you have time to spare, try the four-hour mustang-viewing breakfast ride, where guests and guides ride in search of the elusive wild mustang through some of Nevada's most scenic landscapes. *Reservations required for both rides (702-875-4191).*

The Wild West comes alive at Old Nevada, an 1880's mining town re-created on 115-acre Bonnie Springs Ranch. Nestled in Red Rock Canyon, a 30-minute drive from the Las Vegas Strip, Old Nevada provides plenty of rough-and-tumble action, including gunfights in the streets. There's also a miniature train ride, a wax museum illustrating figures from Nevada's frontier history, a lovely 19C chapel, a restaurant, and shopping for turquoise, silver and Western souvenirs. The petting zoo, housing deer, goats, raccoons, swans, llamas, and even a long-horned steer from Texas, is the most popular attraction on the property. On weekends, stay around for the posse show, an 1830s melodrama in which kids can help track down the mustached villain in an authentically re-created saloon. Of course, there's a public hanging with an obliging stuntman swaying in the wind.

Boulder City★

23mi southeast of Las Vegas via I-93/95 North or I-515 North. 702-293-2034. www.bouldercity.com.

This charming little dry town (no alcohol) is the only city in Nevada that doesn't allow gaming. It was built by the government as a model city, and it has thrived on small-town values that are still very much in evidence today.

Boulder City came into existence circa 1929 to house the workers constructing Hoover Dam and their families. Initially, there was some contention over where the dam was to be built, Boulder Canyon or Black Canyon (where it ended up). Because the Boulder Canyon Project Act had been passed before the location was changed, all plans referred to the Boulder Dam project. So when the Bureau of Reclamation commissioner, Dr. Elwood Mead, personally chose the townsite, he decided to call it Boulder City.

With its location overlooking Lake Mead, Boulder City makes a great base for enjoying all the recreational activities the lake provides. And the city sits just around the corner *(7mi east)* from Hoover Dam. While you're here, relax in the central historic hotel plaza surrounded by eucalyptus trees and water fountains, browse through antique shops along Nevada Highway, or grab a bite at the 1950s-style **Happy Days Diner** *(512 Nevada Hwy.; 702-293-4637)*.

Boulder's Grand Dame

Boris Karloff resided there; Bette Davis vacationed there and Howard Hughes recuperated there after he crashed his plane into Lake Mead. Will Rogers called the hotel home in 1935 when he performed at the Boulder Theatre (where Boulder City resident Desi Arnaz Jr. still puts on productions today).

Built in 1933 to house government and corporate project managers overseeing the building of Hoover Dam, the Dutch Colonial-style **Boulder Dam Hotel** *(1305 Arizona St., Boulder City; 702-293-3510; www.boulderdamhotel.com)* is newly restored to its former glory after an eight-year renovation. Now a B&B, the 22-room lodging was named to the National Register of Historic Places in 1982.

Historic Sites

Spring Mountain Ranch State Park★

15mi west of Las Vegas via Charleston Blvd. 702-875-4141. www.parks.nv.gov/smr.htm. Open year-round daily 8am–dusk. $5.

This 520-acre ranch is located at 3,800ft altitude at the base of the Wilson Cliffs in the Red Rock Canyon National Conservation Area. In the first half of the 19C, this site, with its spring-fed creek and tranquil meadows, was used as a campsite and watering hole by pack and wagon trains headed west along the Spanish Trail. James Wilson, an army sergeant based at Fort Mohave, and his partner George Anderson lay claim to the property in 1876 and named it Sand Stone Ranch. After surviving a long string of owners—including Howard Hughes—the ranch became a state park in 1971.

Visit – The picturesque red main **ranch house** now serves as a visitor center. Acquaint yourself with the area here and then take a self-guided tour through the interior.

More To Do

Outdoor Theater – During June, July and August, outdoor shows are performed at the park by a private production company. Past productions have included *Hello Dolly*, *Oklahoma* and *Smokey Joe's Café*. Bring chairs, blankets and a picnic to enjoy while you're watching the show.

Trail Riding – Silver State Riding Tours rents horses for trail riding in the park *(702-798-7788)*.

A guided tour of the historic area includes the two second-oldest buildings in the Las Vegas Valley: an early 19C blacksmith shop and a sandstone cabin. You'll also see the reservoir created in 1945 by former owner and radio personality Chet Lauck (he dubbed it Lake Harriet for his wife), as well as the gravesites of the Wilson family, who originally homesteaded the property. Periodic living-history demonstrations interpret life on the frontier.

Old Las Vegas Mormon State Historic Park

500 E. Washington Ave. at Las Vegas Blvd. 702-486-3511. www.parks.nv.gov/olvmf.htm. Open year-round daily 8am–4:30pm. $2.

The place where Las Vegas began, this is the site of the first permanent non-native settlement in the Las Vegas Valley. An adobe fort was built along Las Vegas Creek in 1855 by William Bringhurst and 29 of his fellow Mormons, who arrived here from Utah. The outpost, equipped with a post office, served as a way station for travelers making their way along the Spanish Trail to California.

The Mormons tried farming by diverting water from the creek, and even briefly dabbled in mining and smelting after lead was discovered in the mountains to the southwest. But after two years of dissension between two of their leaders, beastly hot weather and periodic Indian raids, the Mormons gave up and abandoned the fort.

In 1865, Octavious D. Gass, a miner from El Dorado Canyon, bought the land and established a small store and blacksmith shop onsite. As the story goes, Gass defaulted on a note in 1881 and the ranch house was taken over by Archibald and Helen Stewart. Even after Archibald was killed in a gunfight in 1884, Helen and her father continued to operate the ranch until 1902, when Helen sold it and the water rights to the San Pedro, Los Angeles & Salt Lake Railroad. The railroad chugged into the valley in 1905, sprouting Las Vegas in its wake. The US Bureau of Reclamation leased and renovated the old fort in 1929 during the construction of Hoover Dam.

What's Left of the Fort?

- **Old Fort** (1855) – The adobe building closest to the creek is the only original part of the Mormons' 150sq ft adobe fort, which featured towers and bastions on the northwest and southeast corners.

- **Ranch House** (1865) – Octavious Gass built this ranch house using part of the Old Fort's foundation.

- **Las Vegas Springs and Creek** – Running through the ranch site is a re-creation of the creek that supplied water to the area. After Las Vegas was founded, the water was diverted there, and the creek dried up.

Museums

It has often been said that good things come in small packages and so it is with Nevada's museums and art galleries. Although Las Vegas is hardly known for its museums, the city has come a long way in presenting some unique, respected and highly informative institutional offerings.

Bellagio Gallery of Fine Art★★

3600 Las Vegas Blvd. S. 702-693-7919. www.bgfa.biz. Open year-round daily 9am–7pm. $15.

With the creation of the Bellagio Gallery of Fine Art, the first gallery on the Strip, it became clear that art in Las Vegas was no longer being given the brush-off. The facility is a noncommercial venue dedicated to presenting high-quality art exhibitions from major national and international museums. It generally brings in two exhibitions a year from the world's greatest art collections, each on display for a period of six months. The gallery offers a self-guided audio tour that's included in the ticket price, so you can stop before any painting and listen to the details about that particular work. The gallery store sells merchandise relating to the various collections.

Chatsworth Collection

In September 2003, the gallery began exhibiting more than 250 works of art from the renowned private collection of the Duke and Duchess of Devonshire. The most historically significant exhibition ever to come to Las Vegas will stay at the gallery through the end of January 2004. It will be followed by **Strictly Monet,** 21 of the Impressionist's paintings lent by the Museum of Fine Art in Boston.

Past Exhibits

- **Andy Warhol: The Celebrity Portraits**—50 portraits and works on paper
- **Alexander Calder: The Art of Invention**
  A group of mobiles, stabiles, toys, jewelry and household objects representing Calder's work between 1926 and 1976.
- **Fabergé: Treasures from the Kremlin**
  200 masterworks by Russian craftsman Peter Carl Fabergé
- **Art in Bloom: The Nature of Impressionism** – Landscape and still-life paintings by the likes of Renoir, Cézanne, Manet and Monet

Guggenheim Hermitage Museum★★

At The Venetian, 3355 Las Vegas Blvd. S. 702-414-2440. www.guggenheimlasvegas.org.
Open year-round daily 9:30am–8:30pm. $15.

From Russia with love has come the 7,660sq ft Guggenheim Hermitage Museum, located off the front lobby of the Venetian. Its opening in October 2001 inaugurated the partnership between the Solomon R. Guggenheim Foundation in New York City and the State Hermitage Museum in St. Petersburg, Russia. Paintings and sculptures exhibited here are drawn from the permanent collections of the State Hermitage Museum, the Guggenheim, and the Kunsthistorisches Museum in Vienna. Exhibitions change approximately twice a year. The works of such artists as Monet, Picasso, van Gogh, van Eyck, Rubens, Titian, Warhol, Rauschenberg and Lichtenstein have been displayed here in the past.

When the Kunsthistorisches Museum entered into an agreement with the Guggenheim and the State Hermitage Museum in January 2001, it united all three institutions in an unprecedented art-world alliance. The Las Vegas museum is operated by the Solomon R. Guggenheim Foundation. Designed by renowned Dutch architect Rem Koolhaas, its stark steel facade is visible from the Strip and contrasts sharply with the architecture around it. Inside, four galleries sport pale maple wood floors and exterior and interior walls of Cor-Ten steel, a material with a dark rusted surface intended to imitate the velvet-covered walls in the 18C galleries at the original Hermitage.

The Real Hermitage

One of the world's great art institutions, Russia's Hermitage Museum occupies five historic buildings—including the Winter Palace, the former home of Russian emperors—set along the river Neva in St. Petersburg. Catherine the Great started the collection in 1764 when she purchased 225 western European paintings. Her core collection grew over the years, added to by her imperial successors to include a wealth of paintings, gemstones and even books.

In 1917, after the fall of the Russian Empire, the Hermitage became a public institution. Today its holdings number some three million objects spanning the centuries from Neolithic sculptures to Picasso paintings.

Museums

The Auto Collections ★

At the Imperial Palace, 3535 Las Vegas Blvd. S. 702-731-3311. www.imperialpalace.com. Open year-round daily 9:30am–9:30pm. $7.

You've got wheels—lots of them—at the Imperial Palace Auto Collection. Regarded as one of the finest collections of its kind in the world, the exhibit showcases more than 750 antique, classic and special-interest vehicles spanning nearly 200 years of automotive history. Of these, more than 200 are on display—and for sale—at any one time in a gallery-like setting on the fifth floor of the Imperial Palace parking facility.

The constantly rotating collection features vehicles once owned by famous and infamous people (James Cagney, Elvis Presley, Al Capone, Benito Mussolini). The collection also displays the rarest and some of the most exclusive and historically significant cars ever produced, including the largest collection of Model I Duesenbergs in the world.

King Tut's Tomb and Museum ★

At Pharaoh's Pavilion in the Luxor, 3900 Las Vegas Blvd. S. 702-262-4000. www.luxor.com. Open year-round Sun–Thu 9am–11pm, Fri & Sat 9am–midnight. $5.

Tut, Tut
You can buy your own cache of collectibles at the museum shop at the exit of King Tut's Tomb and Museum. Here you'll discover replica artifacts, jewelry and art imported from Egypt.

In King Tut's Tomb and Museum at the Luxor all that glitters is still gold. Back in 1922, British archaeologist Howard Carter peered through a small hole into the tomb of King Tutankhamen and spied the magnificent collection of antiquities and treasures representing the finest works of ancient craftsmanship. Carter's discovery turned out to be the archaeological find of all time.

It took Carter 10 years to completely excavate the tomb, and modern-day Egypt six months (and 50 people) to replicate it for the Luxor. King Tut's Tomb and Museum is the only full-scale reproduction of Carter's famous discovery outside Egypt. A self-guided audio tour of the museum allows you to explore the remarkable contents of the fabled tomb, from the young king's sarcophagus to the illustrious guardian statues.

Are They Real?
No, they're replicas of items originally found in Tutankhamen's tomb. Each of the finely crafted works was painstakingly reproduced in Egypt, though, using the same gold leaf and linens, precious pigments, tools, and 3,300-year-old artisan methods.

Madame Tussaud's Celebrity Encounter ★

At The Venetian, 3355 Las Vegas Blvd. S. 702-414-1000. www.venetian.com. Open year-round daily 10am–1:30pm. $19.95.

What do Tom Jones, Wayne Newton, Engelbert Humperdinck, Mick Jagger, Oprah Winfrey, and more than 100 other celebrities have in common? They all have what it takes to get their likeness in the new Madame Tussaud's at the Venetian. When it comes to the making of a star, Madame Tussaud's has broken the mold. About 105–110 masterfully crafted, realistic wax figures of some of the world's most popular film, television, music and sports celebrities, as well as legendary Las Vegas icons, are showcased in the two-story Las Vegas site. At Madame Tussaud's, you can have your picture taken with your favorite

Spirit of America

A $2 million, 2,500sq ft permanent exhibit space that premiered at Madame Tussaud's in October 2002, Spirit of America contains 10 wax portraits of individuals who have had a major impact on America: George Washington, Abraham Lincoln, John F. Kennedy and Jacqueline Kennedy, George W. Bush, Buzz Aldrin and Neil Armstrong, John Wayne, Martin Luther King and Princess Diana.

stars—just don't expect them to get excited about it. As unbelievably lifelike as they look, the only thing real about the figures are their clothes. Most of the celebrities donated garb they have actually worn.

Nevada State Museum ★

700 Twin Lakes Dr. 702-486-5205. http://dmla.clan.lib.nv.us. Open year-round daily 8:30am–4:30pm. Closed Jan 1, Thanksgiving Day & Dec 25. $3.

This museum has a story to tell. That story is Nevada's history and this nationally accredited museum tells it with authority— from a 225-million-year-old ichthyosaur to the Mojave Desert, Native Americans, the mob, and up to modern-day Las Vegas. Located in a pretty park with a duck pond, not far from downtown Las Vegas, the Nevada State Museum's permanent exhibits focus on the natural and

anthropological history of the region. One exhibit you won't want to miss tells the recorded story of "Bugsy" Siegel's Flamingo Hotel—complete with threats on his business partners' lives.

The Liberace Museum

1775 E. Tropicana Ave. 702-798-5595. www.liberace.com. Open year-round Mon–Sat 10am–5pm, Sun 12pm–4pm. Closed Jan 1, Thanksgiving & Dec 25. $12.

Born Wladziu Valentino in Milwaukee, Wisconsin, the acclaimed pianist known as Liberace (1919–1986) first displayed his exceptional talent at the piano at age four. By 1952 Liberace had his own TV show, which won an Emmy for best entertainment program. Two years later, Liberace was earning $2 million for one 26-week season, making him the highest-paid pianist in the world.

Liberace was known for his flash, which lives on in this museum, founded by the entertainer in 1979. Here Liberace's dazzling jewelry, unsurpassed wardrobe, unique pianos—like the rhinestone-covered Baldwin that he played at his last performance at Radio City Music Hall—and custom car collection recall the artist's bigger-than-life persona. Add to the mix Liberace's glitzy 50-pound, 115,000-carat Austrian rhinestone—the largest in the world—given to him as a gift by Swarovski and Company.

Dressed To Thrill

In the Costume Gallery is Liberace's trademark candelabra, along with his famous sequined, jeweled and rhinestone-studded costumes, feathered capes and fur collection. The entertainer favored the black diamond mink lined with more than 40,000 two-and-a-half carat Austrian rhinestones, each one sewn on by hand. Here, too, you'll see his glittering stage jewelry and gold and diamond rings.

Casino Legends Hall of Fame

At the Tropicana, 3801 Las Vegas Blvd. S. 702-739-5444. www.tropicanalv.com. Open year-round daily 9am–9pm. $6.95.

In Las Vegas, legends never die—they end up in the Tropicana's Casino Legends Hall of Fame. The dream of one man, its co-founder and creator, Steve Cutler, the place houses the largest and most unique collection of gaming memorabilia ever assembled. Cutler began amassing his gaming artifacts in 1972 as a dealer at the El Cortez in downtown Las Vegas; today he is considered one of Nevada's leading historians.

More than 738 casinos are represented in the venue, 550 of which no longer exist. From swizzle sticks to slot machines, some 15,000 items trace the evolution of Nevada gaming from its legalization in 1931 to the present day. Here you'll find the largest Nevada gaming-chip collection in existence: more than 8,000 gaming chips in denominations ranging from 1¢ through $100,000.

Las Vegas Art Museum

9600 W. Sahara Ave. 702-360-8000. www.lasvegasartmuseum.org. Open year-round Tue–Sat 11am–5pm, Sun 1pm–5pm. Closed Mon. $5.

By bringing ambitious fine art exhibitions to the community and the city's visitors, the Las Vegas Art Museum, now a Smithsonian affiliate, has further defined the evolving cultural landscape of Las Vegas. What was founded as a community art league in 1950 by dedicated volunteers, has turned into a respected art institution. The exhibition program features internationally recognized artists in all media and time periods. Past exhibitions have featured the work of Chagall, Dalí, Rodin, and contemporary glass artist Dale Chihuly. The museum's small but growing permanent collection includes works by Alexander Calder, Robert Indiana, Larry Rivers and Edward Ruscha.

Las Vegas Natural History Museum

900 Las Vegas Blvd. N. 702-384-3466. www.lvnhm.org. Open year-round daily 9am–4pm. Closed Thanksgiving Day & Dec 25. $6.

It's a shark, it's a dinosaur, it's a good way to combine education and fun through multi-sensory exhibits. The Las Vegas Natural History Museum offers high entertainment value for all ages. Animated exhibits, robotic dinosaurs (including a 35ft-long *Tyrannosaurus rex*), live fish and more than 26 species of taxidermed animals—including rare African water chevrotains (a cross between a pig and a deer) and zebra duikers from Liberia—will take you from the neon jungle of Las Vegas to the real jungle in a flash. There are several "hands-on" areas where animals are brought out to be petted.

One of the entities that put a feather in the city's cap was the Las Vegas showgirl. With her plumed headdresses and long legs, the Vegas showgirl and the lavish productions she appeared in became synonymous with the city in its early years. Alas, the day of the Vegas showgirl is gone, replaced by flashier productions that appeal to an audience weaned on high-tech. But if you hanker for that old-fashioned entertainment, two classic Vegas productions remain.

Folies Bergere★

At the Tropicana, 3801 Las Vegas Blvd. S. 702-739-2411 or 800-829-9034. www.tropicanalasvegas.com. Late show (10pm) is topless; guests must be 16 or older to attend.

Legs, legs, and more legs. Modern audiences have Lou Walters, former entertainment director of the Tropicana (and father of news correspondent Barbara Walters), to thank for introducing Americans to a theatrical form that has been around since 1866. Today the Folies Bergere is the longest continually running show in the US.

In 1975 when the Folies Bergere moved from the Tropicana's Fountain Theatre, where it ran for 16 years, into the new 950-seat Tiffany Theatre, it became an original American production. Every new edition of the show since then has been unique, with new costuming, new production numbers, original choreography and elaborate new stage sets. (To this day, though, the show maintains the historical "Folies" name and is licensed through special arrangement with the original Folies Bergère in Paris.) The latest edition of the Folies Bergere is a contemporary salute to beautiful women through the years, from 1850 to the present. Of course, Jackson kept the award-winning Can-Can, which has been part of the production since 1975.

The First Folies

Paris' first music hall, the glamorous Folies Bergère Theatre, opened in 1869 on the grounds of a 13C monastery. The first nude showgirl appeared on the Folies stage in 1918, changing the show's reputation forever. In the 1920's the Folies began to evolve into a large-scale production. The show reached its pinnacle in the 1930s and 40s, however, when stars such as singer Josephine Baker took the stage.

Donn Arden's Jubilee!

At Bally's Las Vegas, 3645 Las Vegas Blvd S. 702-967-4567 or 800-237-7469.
www.ballyslv.com.

It may have modern-day costumes, sets, sound, lights, choreography and a nearly 100-member cast, but Jubilee! is still a throwback to Las Vegas' Golden Age of lavish stage spectaculars. Having celebrated its 20th anniversary on July 30th, 2001, Jubilee! is the second-longest running show on the Strip, (after Folies Bergere). The quintessential Vegas-style revue was conceived by the late Donn Arden, best known for introducing the Lido de Paris (and the topless showgirl) to the city in the mid-1950s.

When it premiered in 1981 at what was then the MGM Grand, Jubilee! was bigger and more spectacular than any other show on the Strip, and far more expensive. The original staging of Jubilee! cost $10 million. Delilah's jeweled headpiece alone originally cost $3,000 and contained 20 pounds of rhinestones. More than 1,000 costumes are worn during the show, many of them designed by world-renowned designers Bob Mackie and Pete Menefee.

Re-tooled with new costumes, the $3 million opening number now boasts computerized sets, music, special effects, lights and sound. It lasts 16 minutes and is based on Jerry Herman's Hundreds of Girls, featuring 76 performers in extravagant feathered headdresses. In the awesome Ziegfeld Follies-style ending, the entire cast, dressed in jaw-dropping garb, walks down a huge 50-step staircase to the tune of "A Pretty Girl Is Like a Melody." Some things you just can't improve on.

Fun Facts

- 100 different sets require some 100,000 light bulbs and over 125mi of wiring.

- 4,200 pounds of dry ice are used each week to create the fog effects in Jubilee!

- 10 pounds of explosives burst nightly in 50 different pyrotechnical effects.

- During the iceberg scene in the "Titanic" number, 5,000 gallons of recycled water cascade across the stage.

- 8,000mi of sequins, two tons of feathers and 10,000 pounds of jewelry are used in the show.

- The heaviest feathered headdress weighs 35 pounds; the heaviest hat weighs 20 pounds.

Nowhere is Las Vegas' "wow!" factor more apparent than in its production shows. Here are a few of our favorites.

Mystère★

At Treasure Island, 3300 Las Vegas Blvd. S. 702-894-7722 or 800-392-1999. www.treasureisland.com.

If you're hoping to find real treasure at Treasure Island, look no further. It comes in the form of performance without boundaries, ballet without gravity, theater without actors. It's Mystère, the surrealistic celebration of music, dance, acrobatics and comedy from the artistic body that holds the patent on imagination-bending, **Cirque du Soleil** (playing at Treasure Island for an indefinite run).

Though the 72-member cast has taken many circus concepts to unmatched heights in the production, and the theater at Treasure Island is designed to look like an enormous Big Top, any similarity to anything you have ever seen

before ends there. Relying on the performers and their limitless creativity, Mystère presents stunning feats on the trapeze, Korean plank, and Chinese poles as well as aerial bungee ballet.

"O"★

At Bellagio, 3600 Las Vegas Blvd. S. 702-693-7111 or 888-488-7111. www.bellagio.com.

The star of this **Cirque du Soleil** spectacle (playing at Bellagio for an indefinite run) is 1.5 million gallons of water, representing the circle of life. With this mesmerizing show, Cirque's first venture into aquatic theater, the performing-arts company has reached new heights.

From the moment the curtain parts to reveal the forest-like setting on the stage, the mysteries of "O" begin to unfold. Floors disappear into pools of water and walls vanish in the mist. The cast of 74 synchronized swimmers, divers, contortionists and trapeze artists perform incredible feats in and over this liquid stage, which transforms itself from one body of water to another in the space of a few seconds. Actions, not words, tell the story here with perpetual art in motion—and your imagination as the supporting cast.

Here Comes The Sun

What started as a group of talented street performers in the rural community of Baie-Saint-Paul, Quebec in 1982, soon blossomed into a local festival. Two years later, the Cirque du Soleil debuted in the town of Gaspé. With no animals in its ring, Cirque du Soleil is not your run-of-the-mill circus. This outrageous troop aims for a dramatic mix of circus arts and street entertainment set to original music.

MAMMA MIA!

At Mandalay Bay, 3950 Las Vegas Blvd. S. 702-632-7580 or 877-632-7000. www.mandalaybay.com.

ABBA-cadabra. The magic of *MAMMA MIA!*, which opened at Mandalay Bay in February 2003 for a two-year run, is not just in the music and script, but also in the numbers it has pulled out of its hat since its debut in London in 1999. *MAMMA MIA!* ingenuously weaves 22 of the super-group ABBA's songs into a funny and infectious tale of a mother and her soon-to-be-wed daughter. Grossing more than $400 million worldwide to date, the show has broken nearly every box-office record wherever it has played.

Dancing Queens And Kings

A legacy of extraordinary songs, worldwide sales of over 350 million records and the success of films, including *Muriel's Wedding* and *Priscilla: Queen of the Desert*, have ensured ABBA's lasting popularity. By the end of *MAMMA MIA!*, the entire audience is on its feet singing and moving to the music along with the cast, so wear your dancing shoes!

An overnight sensation in London, the production opened to raves in October 2001 at the Wintergarden Theatre on Broadway, where it continues to gross over $1 million a week (pre-show sales of $13 million made it one of the biggest debut successes in Broadway history). There are also sell-out productions in Toronto, Sydney, Tokyo and Hamburg, as well as two national touring companies.

Set in the present day on a tiny, mythical Greek island, *MAMMA MIA!* is a musical love story that crosses continents and generations. The Las Vegas cast is headed by Tina Walsh, who plays Donna, the single mother whose world is turned upside-down by her daughter's wedding. Jill Price (most recently seen in the national tour of *Les Miserables*) plays Sophie, the daughter whose search to find herself and her father lies at the heart of the production.

Frank Sinatra, Dean Martin, Sammy Davis Jr. Big names like these and others built Las Vegas into the "Entertainment Capital of the World." While superstars Tony Bennett, Tom Jones, Engelbert Humperdinck and Barry Manilow still play the city, the latest trend is toward resident headliners who perform long-term in their own showrooms, such as "Mr. Las Vegas," Wayne Newton, or the newest headliner, Celine Dion.

Celine Dion

At Caesars Palace, 3570 Las Vegas Blvd. S. 702-731-7110 or 877-423-5463. www.celinedion.com.

On March 25th, 2003, A New Day premiered in the new $95-million Colosseum at Caesars Palace. From its very first dawning, it has been a much-heralded event, allowing its star, Celine Dion, who will perform in the show for three years, to present herself to audiences in a brand new light.

Given this opportunity to shine, Dion has entered a different stage of her career—literally, on the 22,450sq ft proscenium that is one of the largest stages in the world, and figuratively, as this is the first time she has been part of a major theatrical production. In the process, Dion's talent is being harnessed in a new direction. Although she's sold more than 155 million albums worldwide—making her the biggest selling female artist of all time—she hopes that the show will guide her to self-discovery, push the limits of her performance and offer a new stage experience to her devoted fans.

It's A New Day

Produced by Concerts West and presented by Chrysler, A New Day seeks to heighten and intensify the senses so that each spectator leaves the show seeing more than they did the day before. Each song is its own vignette and the unique spectacle of song, theatre, dance and state-of-the-art technology surrounding Dion, who is on stage at all times, features the largest indoor LED screen in North America. The scenes and images projected on it create an extraordinary illusion of depth and transcend the usual physical limitations of the stage.

Clint Holmes

At Harrah's Las Vegas, 3475 Las Vegas Blvd. S. 702-369-5222 or 800-634-6765. www.netwebsite.com/clintholmes.

It was in 1973 that singer/ entertainer Clint Holmes began his climb up the show-business ropes when he re-corded a song called "Play-ground In My Mind." The single, on the Epic label, became an international hit in 1974, selling two-and-a-half million copies around the world.

Today Holmes is a major Vegas player making his way up in the main-room arena. He performs on a nightly basis at Harrah's with a contract through January 2006 and a showroom named after him. In an eclectic, ener-getic, funny and emotionally moving show, Holmes slides from pop into jazz, Broadway, opera, contemporary tunes and more, with his silky smooth vocal stylings.

Along with the music is a touching and witty personal glimpse into the life of this artist, who is the product of an interracial marriage. With his musical conductor Bill Fayne, nine band members, and a female back-up singer, Holmes' singing, dancing and warm comedic touch turns the playground in his mind into the reality ride of the evening.

In Like Clint

The multifaceted entertainer has shared co-billing with Bill Cosby, Joan Rivers and Don Rickles in Las Vegas in the 1980s. He also did a stint as Rivers' sidekick and as an announcer on *The Late Show*. A former correspondent for *Entertainment Tonight*, Holmes hosted his own Emmy-winning talk/variety show on WOR, *New York at Night*.

What's different about Holmes' show is that it's personal. He performs some original material that's autobiographical, which he wrote with musician Nelson Kole. After spending an evening with Holmes, you leave the show actually knowing something about him. Holmes believes it's that personal touch that resonates. That's why people often approach him after a performance to tell him how much they liked a particular song about his family. And that's why talking is as much a part of his show as singing.

Gladys Knight

*At Flamingo Las Vegas, 3555
Las Vegas Blvd. S. 702-733-3333
or 800-221-7299.
www.flamingolasvegas.com.*

When one of America's longtime favorite singers debuted her indefinite stay at the Flamingo Las Vegas in February 2002, it was undoubtedly a Knight to remember. That's because for popular entertainer Gladys Knight, who performed her first Las Vegas main-room engagement with the Pips at the Flamingo back in 1968, life has come full circle. A Las Vegas resident for nearly 25 years, Knight is living her dream come true. Her indefinite engagement allows her to have a family life while giving her an opportunity to reach her fans, whom she considers as extended family.

In terms of the show, which is produced by DGCL (Las Vegas entertainer Danny Gans and his manager, Chip Lightman), Knight always performs her most popular music, along with other songs. And she does her best to wrap it all up in an entertaining package, injecting "a little pizzazz here, a little production value there," as she puts it. Knight wants her audience to have that comforting feeling that they had when they were young and came home from school to the smell of fresh-baked cookies—the feeling that said "Mom's home."

Heard It Through The Grapevine

Born in 1944 in Atlanta, Georgia, Gladys Knight made her solo singing debut at age four at a Baptist church. Her train toward stardom left the station in 1952 after eight-year-old Knight won a prize on the Ted Mack Amateur Hour. Shortly thereafter she formed a group called the Pips with her brother and sister and two cousins providing harmonies to Knight's throaty vocals. The group eventually signed with Motown Records and made their first big hit with Marvin Gaye's song, "I Heard It Through the Grapevine."

Gladys Knight and the Pips rode the pop charts through the 1970s and 80s. In 1988 the group cut their last album, *All Our Love*, together. The following year, Knight left the Pips to pursue a solo career.

Rita Rudner

At New York-New York, 3790 Las Vegas Blvd. S. 702-740-6815 or 800-963-9634. www.ritarudner.com.

To most people, doing a nightly live stage show, having your own daily television show, writing a book, and being a wife and new mother all at the same time would be enough to make you bonkers.

Comedienne Rita Rudner, who performs in New York-New York's Cabaret Theatre seven nights a week, *is* doing it all. Wife to writer/producer Martin Bergman and mother to adopted daughter, Molly, Rudner does her own syndicated weekday TV show and is working on another book *(Tickled Green)*. Meanwhile, her pet canine, aptly named Bonkers (after her grandfather, Rudner claims), works like a dog for a few minutes each night in her stage show as Rudner unleashes her talents on a waiting world. With shows every night of the week (two on Saturday), Rudner consistently sells out the 451-seat theater.

Actually, Rudner gets her own chance to wag the dog on *Ask Rita*, a lively ad-lib panel discussion about relationships and personal problems. There's a possibility that the TV show, which is currently being filmed in Los Angeles, may move to Las Vegas to be filmed in front of a live audience—which means that you could have the opportunity to attend.

Packing A Punch Line

While Rudner admits that it's never easy to come up with new material, she tries every night to introduce one new thought. If she's lucky, she'll get one or two jokes a week that she's very proud to weave into her act.

Rudner writes all her own material, focusing on relationship humor and common experiences, jotting her thoughts down in notebooks that she reviews a half-hour before the show. Always on the lookout for new ideas, Rudner says that when someone pulls on a door that says "Push," she knows there's material for comedy there—after all, she's done it herself a million times.

The Scintas

At Rio, 3700 W. Flamingo Rd. 702-777-7777 or 888-746-7784. www.scintas.com.

The Rio serves up sibling revelry on a nightly basis in the Rio's Scintas Showroom. That's Scinta (pronounced SHIN-tah) as in Joe, Frank, and Christine (Chrissi) Scinta, along with adopted cohort Peter O'Donnell. During the evening, you may hear tales of other relatives—Grandpop Kunta Scinta, Uncle Fulla Scinta, and Aunt Stepina Pila Scinta—they like to keep things all in the family.

The Family Business

To sum up the Scintas' 90-minute act in a few words, Joe is on bass and does a right-on Mick Jagger as well as playing comedic foil to younger brother Frank. Frank plays virtually every instrument (self-taught), does a range of impressions that brings down the house, then takes on Peter O'Donnell (the only non-Sicilian Scinta) for the ultimate comedic percussion duet. Enter younger sister Chrissi, who lights up the stage with her powerful soprano voice.

Of course, it's hard to know what to expect from an act that was categorized by one entertainment critic as a cross between the Village People, Don Rickles and Cher. One thing's for certain—no one is exempt from being picked on. At the end of the night, though, you'll leave reassured that the Scinta family loves their audiences as much as they love performing.

All who have seen the act agree that it's not just their tremendously talented combination of music, comedy and impressions (complete with wigs and props) that has put the group at the hub of Las Vegas. It's also their habit of

tugging at the heartstrings of their audiences with their obvious family devotion, stories and songs.

The Scintas have never been scripted; they simply go out on stage and have fun in their own unique way. If you have any doubt, the production number in the beginning of the show reflects the true image of who the Scintas are: they're family first, then singers and comedians.

Wayne Newton

At the Stardust, 3000 Las Vegas Blvd. S. 702-617-5577 or 888-217-9565.
www.waynenewton.com.

Many years ago, Sammy Davis Jr. said to Wayne Newton: "When people come to Las Vegas, there are two things that people have to see—Hoover Dam and Wayne Newton, and not necessarily in that order." Well, it seems that little has changed. Each year, thousands of people flock to see Hoover Dam and Wayne Newton, and *not* necessarily in that order. In fact, if anything, the big dam is beginning to pale in comparison to the floodgates that have opened where Newton's career is concerned.

Offers for interviews, movies and TV just keep pouring in. All this activity has coincided with the lucrative ten-year deal that Newton signed in January 2000 with the Stardust Hotel & Casino. Under the terms of the contract, Newton will perform at the hotel 40 weeks a year until 2010, and the Stardust named its theater after him.

Call Ahead

Wondering if you'll have time for dinner before the show starts? It's best to call the box office 3hrs before the posted showtime to see when the headliner is expected to take the stage. You don't want to give up that gourmet dinner for an opening act.

Newton (born in 1942) was 15 when he began performing in 1959 with his brother, Jerry, in the lounge of the Fremont Hotel. His first solo headliner booking came in 1963 at the Flamingo. After that, he settled in and became a mainstay in Las Vegas entertainment, earning the moniker "Mr. Las Vegas" and logging in some 25,000 performances in the city by February 1997.

Great Imposters

Some of Las Vegas' favorite performers just aren't themselves these days. They're everyone from Elvis to Neil Diamond to Kermit the Frog. However, while the performers may have multiple personalities, it's you who, luckily, will be hearing voices.

American Superstars

At The Stratosphere, 2000 Las Vegas Blvd. S. 702-380-7777 or 800-998-6937. www.stratlv.com.

American Superstars, the celebrity impersonation show at the Stratosphere since April 1996, got a makeover for the new Millennium. In the process, it took on a whole new personality—Elvis—who after having left it some time ago, is now back in the building, in a manner of speaking.

Mark Callas, executive producer of the show, and his partner, Donny Lee Moore, hadn't counted on a sighting of the King at all. There hadn't been an Elvis in American Superstars since the show initially opened in Vegas at the Flamingo Hilton in 1993. After the Hilton, the show went on to the Luxor, sans Elvis, from 1995 to 1997, and then opened at the Stratosphere (again without Elvis) in December 1997. Where public opinon was concerned, however, the King's absence from these venues was turning these properties into "heartbreak hotels."

The show's repeat customers clamored for Elvis, who is definitely alive in Las Vegas thanks to any number of impersonators. So, at the beginning of 2000, when the producers decided to refocus the show towards American pop icons, Elvis was brought back and he's been a smash hit ever since.

Since they're audience favorites, the acts in American Superstars don't change that often. Everyone sings live, emulating the superstars they portray in voice, dress and mannerisms.

Playing Among The Stars

American Superstars recently added an impression of the hard-rockin' Texas band ZZ Top to its lineup of musical celebrity tributes. The show includes Kevin Curry on guitar portraying Billy Gibbons, Dan Stover on bass as Dusty Hill and Craig Aaron Small on drums filling in for Frank Beard. ZZ Top catapulted to superstardom during the video music era.

Danny Gans

At The Mirage (see Casinos), 3400 Las Vegas Blvd. S. 702-791-7111 or 800-627-6667. www.dannygans.com.

One look at Danny Gans on stage and it's easy to see why he has become the Vegas ideal. He's talented, he's witty, and he's just loaded with personalities—nearly 300 of them, to be exact. Not to mention that he's always the lives of the party, the one he invites people to attend nightly in The Danny Gans Theatre at the Mirage. He opened here in April 2000 to consistently sold-out crowds.

Nicknamed "the man of a thousand voices," Danny Gans is truly a man for all ages. Chronological ages, that is. His show, which is different every night, offers about 100 fast-paced impressions of singing stars and actors from every age group and era, leaving no tone unturned. The crowd doesn't even seem to mind that every so often, when Gans opens his mouth to sing, he obviously has a little frog in his throat. Not to worry, it's only Kermit. Like his Muppet friend, Gans has found his own "rainbow connection" with his audiences.

Gans' show offers an entire spectrum of entertainment, taking people from the 1940s with favorites Frank Sinatra, Tony Bennett and Nat King Cole to current recording artists such as John Meyer, Macy Gray and Dave Matthews. In his emotional rendition of Bruce Springsteen's "The Rising," Gans not only sings as Bruce but plays the guitar, too. His acting piece, which includes scenes from *On Golden Pond*, *Rocky*, *Forrest Gump* and *Scent of a Woman*, has garnered raves from the likes of Sylvester Stallone, Kevin Costner and Dustin Hoffman.

Gee, That's Funny!

Gans feels that in his show, humor is everything. The majority of the show is funny, so that when Gans gets serious—talking about his family, doing a tribute to Sarah Vaughan, Billie Holiday and Sammy Davis Jr., or portraying sad moments from the movies—those bits stand out in relief.

Frank Marino

At the Riviera, 2901 Las Vegas Blvd. S. 702-734-5110 or 800-634-6753. www.frankmarino.com.

You could say that for nearly half of his 40 years, life has been a drag for Frank Marino. He stars nightly as comedienne Joan Rivers in An Evening at La Cage.

Frankly Speaking

Marino gets some of his material from some very unique sources. When it comes to the designs for his gowns, 90 percent of the time he dreams up the ideas and the rest come from some offbeat sources. One of those places is from the Barbie doll, which the impersonator claims has the best fantasy dresses. Marino quips that he is actually a copy of Barbie, "the only one who has more plastic parts than him."

Celebrating his 18th anniversary with the famed female impersonation show in September 2003, Marino has always been "one of the guys who's one of the girls." There's no denying that Marino, who's had more than $100,000 worth of plastic surgery, looks better in an evening gown than most women. Now he's ready to come out of the closet, the one that holds his extravagant wardrobe and jewelry, and be perfectly frank about what it takes to be a woman in a man's world—Can we talk?

Marino makes 17 costume changes a night. His closet contains more than two thousand gowns, which range in price from $1,000 to $5,000 apiece, and he pays for every one himself. Designed mainly by costume king Bob Mackie, Marino's wardrobe has become such a trademark over the years that people come to the show just to see his new outfits. Currently, he only opens the show as Joan Rivers, doing the rest of the changes as a glamorous femme fatale character he created himself.

Frank Marino has been voted "Best Dressed in Las Vegas" four times. It's no wonder with what he has to choose from:

- 2,000 evening gowns
- 50 wigs
- A trunk full of jewelry
- 300 pairs of shoes

Jay White: America's Neil Diamond Tribute

At the Riviera, 2901 Las Vegas Blvd. S. 702-734-5110 or 800-634-6753.
www.neilzircon.com.

A diamond has many facets but none have gotten more points for authenticity than Jay White, who portrays Neil Diamond nightly in the Riviera's Le Bistro Theatre. White shines in his portrayal of the rock superstar, as evidenced by Neil Diamond himself who, in an August 2001 interview, called White his "favorite tribute performer." In April 2003, White was lauded as "Outstanding Performance–Concert Stage" at the 12th Annual Reel Awards in Los Angeles, which brings together the best celebrity impersonators from all over the world.

White first became a Neil Diamond fan back in the mid-1970s. Diamond's "Love at the Greek" album had just been released and while listening to it one day, White became aware that he liked every song on the LP. He began buying Diamond's records and singing along with them at home.

Soon White discovered that his and Diamond's vocal ranges were the same and that his natural sound was very similar to that of the superstar. Around 1979, White got together with a guy at a party who was putting together an a cappella singing group. They called themselves The Voices and started performing 1950s and 60s songs on the weekends in bars in Detroit, where White grew up. Because he was a Neil Diamond fan, he would perform three or four Diamond songs solo, accompanying himself on acoustic guitar. That was the beginning of a successful career.

Will The Real Jay White Please Stand Up?

Even though he may resemble Neil Diamond in real life, White says that when he leaves the stage, the persona ends there.

Onstage, however, his brain is totally focused on just being Neil Diamond. To White, it's more than just looking and sounding like Diamond. The facial expressions and body language are as important as getting the voice right; they bring realism to what he does. It's all become second nature now to the entertainer who says he feels like Neil Diamond, not Jay White, when he's performing.

Legends In Concert

At the Imperial Palace, 3535 Las Vegas Blvd. S. 702-731-3311 or 800-634-6441. www.imperialpalace.com.

Frank Sinatra still comes around to perform; Richie Valens pops in to entertain; and Elvis has not left the building in two decades. They join a host of legends—those who have passed on as well as those who are still with us—who are being brought to life nightly in the Imperial Palace's celebrity tribute show, Legends In Concert®, which celebrated its 20th anniversary in May 2003.

Considered the granddaddy of the live-star impersonation shows, Legends in Concert is not only the original, but is the largest of these shows in the world. Conceived and created by John Stuart, what began as a six-week booking into the hotel in May 1983 has turned into a two-decade run. This award-winning flagship production is the longest-running, independently produced production show in Las Vegas today.

Legends In The Making

Not all the acts in the show have appeared in a major production before. If performers have the look and mannerisms of a particular star and have experience, producers will work with them. They'll also send people to makeup artists and dentists and show them pictures of the respective stars as well as suggest clothing they should wear. Particular attention is paid to the era of the celebrity being portrayed; hair, make-up and style of dress must be accurate to the period.

The show changes every three months. The list of nearly 100 legends portrayed over the years includes Marilyn Monroe, Buddy Holly, Madonna, Jerry Lee Lewis, The Beatles, Dean Martin, Aretha Franklin, Jennifer Lopez and Bing Crosby.

Legends in Concert seeks to portray stars with wide appeal. That objective is carried out by singers, dancers, musicians and comedians who have the uncanny ability to re-create the presence of these great entertainers using their own voices and looks.

Now you see them; now you see them again and again and again. Las Vegas' resident headliner magicians have something up their sleeves indeed—tigers, women, birds, rocket ships and knives, to name a few. Faster than speeding bullets, able to leap tall reputations in a single bound, they are the supermen of the magic scene.

Amazing Johnathan

At the Flamingo Las Vegas, 3555 Las Vegas Blvd S. 702-733-3333 or 800-221-7299. www.amazingj.com.

Seeing is believing, and nowhere is that truer than at the Flamingo, where the Amazing Johnathan appears nightly. From the moment the comedic magician walks out on stage, he offers a crystal-clear, streak-free picture of bizarrely funny—even if he's not, at that particular moment, gulping down Windex.

With his bonafide don't-try-this-at-home act billed as "where magic and comedy collide," Johnathan focuses his impact on getting laughs. Nightly packed houses watch Johnathan eat razor blades, put a knife through his arm, put a pencil in his ear and out his nose, and swig Windex. Now, even without the help of his trusty assistant, the Psychic Tanya, Johnathan himself can see clearly into the future. And he's going to keep people laughing for a long time to come.

By his own admission, the 43-year-old Johnathan is as edgy and as politically incorrect as he can be. But he emphasizes that it's all in jest; he doesn't cross the line from funny to mean-spirited. His fast, furious and extremely funny approach has earned him rave reviews. *Rolling Stone* magazine refers to him as "one of the best comics working today." Among his honors, he is a two-time winner of the International Magic Award for "Best Comedy Magician."

It's Amazing

There are two real magic tricks in the Amazing Johnathan's show—the rest is spoof.

Each of his shows is preceded by interactive audience comedy (via a live video camera and a *big* screen) and a different comedy or magic opening act weekly. During each show, Johnathan always brings up a "willing" participant on stage to assist him.

Parents beware: Johnathan does use profanity in his performance.

Lance Burton

At the Monte Carlo, 3770 Las Vegas Blvd. S.
702-730-7160 or 877-386-8224.
www.lanceburton.com

Lance Burton was just five years old when he became acquainted with an illusion called the "Miser's Dream." He was called up on stage by magician Harry Collins, who proceeded to pull silver dollars from behind the young boy's ear, his nose, under his chin and out of thin air. Collins then put the silver dollars into a large bucket, which soon overflowed with coins.

Poof! It's Magic

Burton, who admits that it's the plot or concept that he looks for in deciding whether to do an illusion (he likes something with an interesting twist at the end), has become a master at putting his own mark on the magic he performs. The magician tries not to categorize his style and claims his illusion-creating is a "mysterious process"—even to him!

Of course, all that was just a drop in the bucket compared to the magical empire Burton would conjure up years later. But for the master magician, who still has six years left on his initial 13-year contract with the Monte Carlo, that one moment of magic changed his life. Burton's goal in doing magic is to give the audience the same feeling he had when he was that five-year-old boy.

What's Up Burton's Sleeve?

- **Dove Act** – This famous act brought Burton to prominence. Burton makes doves appear and disappear, and vanish into handkerchiefs and candles.
- **Six-Pack** – Six beautiful showgirls come out of one suitcase in succession.
- **Floating Birdcage** – A birdcage holding Elvis the parakeet floats in mid-air three or four feet from Burton and then floats back.
- **The Flying Car** – A white Corvette flies in thin air, disappears, then reappears.
- **Sword Fight** – Burton's finale is a fencing match in which the magician fights a villain. It looks like the bad guy kills Burton, but when the villain takes off his mask—voila!—it *is* Burton!

Penn & Teller

At the Rio, 3700 W. Flamingo Rd. 702-777-7777 or 888-746-7784. www.pennandteller.com.

The bad boys of magic, Penn & Teller always strive to make their audiences feel at home. That's because for this magical duo, home is where the wood chipper, handcuffs, razor blades, guns, and other props of their act are—it's wise to stay awake for this one!

Penned and Teller-All

Penn & Teller have penned three best-selling books, *Cruel Tricks for Dear Friends*, *How to Play with Your Food* and *How to Play In Traffic*. Their latest project is a new series for the Showtime network.

Luckily, home for Penn & Teller is at the Rio these days, where they have signed to perform through 2004 (and the hotel happily cleans up the blood). The duo refers to themselves as "a couple of eccentric guys who have learned how to do a few cool things." Others have called them "pure entertainment and de-mented originality" *(Newsweek)*; "two of the funniest people alive" *(Entertainment Weekly)*; and "evil geniuses" (David Lettermen). However you view it, what you see is what you get with this pair.

Together since 1975, Penn & Teller are so-called "swindlers and scam artists" who perform tricks (and scams) with rather threatening props, not to mention the occasional bunny in a wood chipper. Their unique brand of magic and bizarre comedy includes throwing knives at attractive females in the audience, eating fire with a showgirl, transforming a wayward girl into an 800-pound gorilla; and hanging Penn by the neck while Teller does hand shadows. Vegas audiences force the pair to keep sharpening up their old tricks and coming up with new, more spectacular stunts. One can only imagine.

Magic Shows

Siegfried & Roy At The Mirage

3400 Las Vegas Blvd. S. 702-792-7777 or 800-392-1999. www.themirage.com.

They say they'd rather be called storytellers than magicians. For sure, world-renowned illusionists Siegfried & Roy have one tall tale to tell. They've given 5,800 shows in 13 years, brought in box-office receipts that have topped the billion-dollar mark, and entertained more than 10 million people. Not to mention they helped preserve two nearly extinct species—white tigers and white lions. After recently signing a lifetime contract with the Mirage, the duo cemented their position as the longest, most successful continuously running entertainers in the history of Las Vegas. You could say that the Magicians of the Century have truly got the tiger by the tail.

SARMOTI

Siegfried & Roy were the first to successfully put magic on the Strip, ultimately turning "Sin City" into what could easily be called Sarmoti City. "Sarmoti" is an acronym for Siegfried & Roy: Masters of the Impossible.

As the Empire State Building is to New York City, so are Siegfried & Roy to Las Vegas, having become synonymous with the city as a number-one entertainment destination. It's been said that their contribution to magic is indefinable.

Where The Wild Things Are

It was animal magnetism that drew Siegfried & Roy together in the first place, and it is conservation of two extinct-in-the-wild species—white tigers and white lions—that still motivates them.

The illusionists' camaraderie with their Royal white tigers and white lions has become their trademark. For years, Siegfried & Roy have worked to protect and preserve these endangered animals through global awareness and breeding programs established on three continents in association with the Zoological Society of Cincinnati in Ohio, the Johannesburg Zoological Gardens in South Africa, and Hollywood Park in Stukenbrock, Germany. Thanks to the daring duo, there are now 39 Royal white tigers and 23 white lions in existence, most of them in Nevada.

Siegfried and Roy notably do things a little differently where their show is concerned. Aware that the world has long been fascinated by magic, they have chosen to work their own brand of magic alongside their magnificent wild animals: white tigers and lions, leopards, a panther and an elephant. The performers aim to give the audience a vicarious chance to commune with nature.

The animals, not the humans, are the star performers in Seigfried & Roy's act. Seigfried calls the beasts their "co-stars," noting that he and Roy couldn't perform magic without the animals' talent, intelligence, and comradeship.

It's the combination of Roy's unfathomable rapport with exotic and mammoth animals coupled with Siegfried's mastery of magic and illusions that has resulted in the original art form that has become their show. Their elaborate theatrical spectacle has been called "a seamless compilation of Pink Floyd, Houdini, Rousseau, Wagner, Barnum, *Fantasia*, *Peter Pan* and *A Midsummer's Night Dream*." It costs an astonishing $35 million to produce.

While Siegfried & Roy say that their greatest satisfaction comes from creating a nightly once-in-a-lifetime, dare-to-believe-your-eyes experience for their audiences, they themselves still marvel at the daily opportunity they have to stand side-by-side with their animals on stage. They consider working with the animals to be a privilege. When an animal—from a tiny kitten to a huge Asian elephant—gives its trust, it's the greatest gift in the world.

Siegfried & Roy's Signature Illusion

• Making Gilda, a 4-ton elephant, magically disappear and reappear.

If you enjoy being the life of the party, or at the very least, not just being a passive observer, then these two shows are the place to be.

Ba-Da-Bing

Sazio's at the Orleans, 4500 W. Tropicana Ave. 702-285-5399. www.orleanscasino.com.

If you have an appetite for a good time, Ba-Da-Bing is a great new casino experience. The interactive dinner show at the Orleans is truly a family affair. The Spaghetti Family, the Linguini Family, the Antipasto Family and the Pizza Family will ensure that guests *will* get their just desserts celebrating the birthday of the Las Vegas Godfather, Mr. Big—even if Cousin Vinnie has them slightly under the gun. Ba-Da-Bing.

Birthdays Can Be Murder
At this party, you might get frisked by one of Mr. Big's gun-toting goombas, witness a murder, or dance the Tarantella and sing. Why, one of you could even turn out to be Mr. Big himself. For those who would rather observe than participate, you can buy a general-admission seat, which allows you to just eat and watch.

The new sensation at the hotel, which takes place in famed chef Gustav Mauler's wonderful Italian restaurant, Sazio's, is a comedic barrel of tongue-in-cheek fun as goombas, gangsters, mayhem and murder run rampant amidst a delicious three-course meal (Caesar salad, a choice of one of four entrées, dessert and champagne).

As with every self-respecting mob scene, there is lots of singing and dancing. Not to mention that you might find yourself sitting next to a gangster at dinner or end up as part of the action yourself as the cast tries to find a moll for the BadAssio Brothers, who allegedly have infiltrated the party and have a contract out for Mr. Big.

Upon being seated in Sazio's 80-seat private dining room, you'll lose your own identity and become a member of one of the above-named Italian *famiglias*. A Don is chosen from each table to represent that family, and, of course, to sign a cease-fire agreement for the party's duration.

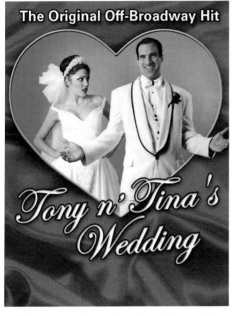

The Original Off-Broadway Hit

Tony n' Tina's Wedding

Tony 'n' Tina's Wedding

At the Rio, 3700 W. Flamingo Rd. 702-777-7777 or 800-752-9746. www.playrio.com.

Tony 'n' Tina's Wedding is a play about a wedding, not an elopement, but that hasn't stopped the hilarious interactive production from becoming a runaway hit. Ever since the show opened (appropriately on February 14, 2002) in the Rio's Calypso Tent for a long-term run, guests have been eating, drinking, dancing and mingling with Tony and Tina and their family and friends. Make no mistake about it, the hilarious antics will have you rolling in the aisle—before, during, and after the wedding party marches down it.

The production, which has run in 30 major cities since its inception 15 years ago, is concurrently playing in nine other locations besides Las Vegas. Boasting a cast of 26 and a live three-piece band under the supervision of Vita Corindi, the show is 25 percent scripted and 75 percent ad-lib. The thread that runs through it is a generations-old rift between the families of Tina Vitale and Tony Nunzio that comes to the fore at their Italian-American wedding—kind of a Romeo and Juliet meets the Godfather.

As you enjoy the wedding and then busy yourself at the reception mentally playing "guess which cast member's coming to dinner," you'll partake in a real buffet-style meal of salads, pastas, a chicken dish, vegetables, garlic bread, and wedding cake. And don't forget the champagne toast!

The Engagement

Tony n' Tina's Wedding was conceived by Nancy Cassaro and created by a group of actors who called themselves Artificial Intelligence. The idea for the play was sparked after Cassaro ended up attending four weddings in two weekends. Though it opened at Carmelita's, a Cuban wedding hall on 14th Street in New York, in 1988, the show never had an actual script until 1994.

With its bright lights, glitz and glitter, Las Vegas has always been looked upon as a late-night town. But lately, many headliners are saying it's about time—1pm & 3pm or 2pm & 4pm—to do afternoon shows.

Mac King

At Harrah's, 3475 Las Vegas Blvd. S. 702-369-5222 or 800-634-6765. www.mac-king.com.

If comedy-magic is your bag, then the Mac King Show, appearing afternoons in the Improv theater at Harrah's, is something you won't want to miss. King's unique act is not your run-of-the-mill magic show; it contains an unusual combination of quirky humor, visual gags, and amazing sleights of hand. It's serious magic delivered in a hilarious tongue-in-cheek manner.

Besides making his head disappear inside a paper bag, King catches live goldfish out of the air, finds an audience member's playing card in a sealed box of cereal, and transforms himself into Siegfried & Roy and then transforms Siegfried & Roy into a white tiger. Of course, the audience is invited to participate. After the show, you can find King outside selling T-shirts and chatting with people.

King is known for his engaging personality and original illusions. Among them is his infamous Cloak of Invisibility, an ordinary yellow raincoat that possesses "extraordinary" powers. King convinces the audience that this coat renders him invisible. The hilarious gag that follows involves astounding illusory feats.

The comedic magician also tosses his cookies between the magical states of "now you see them" and "now you don't." King's affinity for Fig Newtons is a recurring running sight gag in the show; the cookies seem to appear in the most unlikely places and situations throughout his performance and disappear in the same manner.

King's Credits

King has appeared on seven NBC magic specials and holds the distinction of being the only performer to have performed on all five of NBC's World's Greatest Magic shows. He was most recently seen in the Travel Channel's special Magic Road Trip, which aired in Summer 2003, and in the documentary Now That's Funny, released by Tricoast Studios in the latter part of 2003.

Rick Thomas

At the Tropicana, 3801 Las Vegas Blvd. S. 702-739-2417 or 800-829-9034.
www.rick@rickthomas.com.

Labeled the most successful afternoon show in the history of Las Vegas, much of the popularity of Rick Thomas: The Art of Dreaming stems from the fact that it's a nighttime-caliber show being presented during the day.

Before the Tropicana, Thomas had always performed at night. So he created a show that could play at night in any venue—it was never designed as a daytime production. Thomas maintains that once the doors of the showroom close and the show begins, it doesn't matter what time it is.

Accompanied on stage by four beautiful dancers and four Royal Bengal tigers, Thomas delights in doing things not done before on the Strip. A lot of the illusions in his act, which he designed, have been built strictly for him. He begins his show with his bird act called Out of Thin Air, for which he was named "Stage Magician of the Year" at the World Magic Awards in 2000.

Tricks of the Trade

The following is a sampling of the unique tricks Thomas pulls out of the air:

Out of Thin Air – Doves are produced from thin air; a bright flash of light turns into a cockatoo; a silk scarf floats across the stage and becomes a cockatoo, and lots more.

Taking It To The Street – Dressed in a black leather jacket, Thomas stands on a platform across two sawhorses when, all of a sudden, a motorcycle appears between his legs.

Dance, Float, Fly – In his signature illusion, a double levitation, Thomas causes his female assistant to float 18ft up into the air. He then magically flies up to meet her before he makes her disappear into thin air.

Mardi Gras – In this stunning finale, four different-colored silk banners put into a box become four women dressed in the same colors. Four tigers also appear in mid-air.

Ronn Lucas

At Rio, 3700 W. Flamingo Rd. 702-777-7777 or 888-746-7784. www.ronnlucas.com.

The Rio's afternoon performer offers guests a unique invitation to put their money where his mouth is. For the mere price of a ticket, those in the Masquerade Showroom at 3pm *(except Tue)* will get to meet Ronn Lucas, aka "The Man Who Can Make Anything Talk." Audiences will also be introduced to his mouthpieces, including Buffalo Billy, Scorch the Dragon, a wise-cracking microphone stand, an unruly bright green sock, and other "found" objects. Rest assured, these entities will be receiving no-lip service from Lucas, pegged by both the New York Times and the London Times as "the world's best ventriloquist."

Mindful that he is creating an illusion of life by carrying on a conversation with a separate entity, Lucas challenges his audiences at the top of each show. He tells the crowd that his goal is to fool them, that he wants to be so good that they will think his puppets are alive and that he'll have to remind them that they're not.

While there are no strings attached—to either Lucas' puppets or act—it is his astonishing vocal manipulation that has been praised around the globe. Lucas can make a basketball yodel while he blows up a balloon, and trade jokes with his own microphone. He can even make a toaster sing both rounds of "Row, Row, Row Your Boat" simultaneously.

Alter Egos

Without question, Buffalo Billy and Scorch are dummies extraordinaire. Lucas claims that they are his alter egos, with Billy being the precocious kid that he always wanted to be, and Scorch being the teenager inside of him—the adolescent ball of energy that's full of excitement and false bravado. The other characters reflect facets of Lucas' personality as well. Yes, even the unsuspecting audience member, cajoled up on stage by Lucas—who turns him or her into a full-size talking, singing and dancing dummy—is forced to surrender to Lucas' humorous take on things.

WEDDING CHAPELS

If you're looking for other ways to kill an afternoon in Vegas, maybe you should try getting married. After all, there aren't too many life-changing experiences you can enjoy for $55 these days. That's what a marriage license costs from the Clark County Marriage License Bureau *(200 S. Third St., bottom level of Clark County Courthouse; 702-455-4416; parental consent required if under 18)*. And with some 50 chapels in the Las Vegas area, including one (or more) in each of the major hotels, an average of 300 couples per day take their vows in the city.

The state's liberal marriage laws require no waiting period and no blood tests. For those who wish to go the no-frills route, another $50 will get you married by the marriage commissioner, who can be found in offices across the street from the courthouse.

Wedding chapels in the Strip resorts feature something for every taste and pocketbook (want Elvis as your best man?). The independent chapels on the Strip, from the Little Church of the West *(4617 Las Vegas Blvd. S.)* to the dozens of chapels past Sahara Avenue on the way downtown, can provide your heart's desire in terms of weddings. If you're really pressed for time, tie the knot at the Little White Wedding Chapel's 24-hour drive-through window, called The Tunnel of Vows *(1301 Las Vegas Blvd.)*.

Some Vegas residents are just tailor-made for life in the "Neon Jungle." They love the bright lights and know how to claw their way to the top. And they work for food!

The Lion Habitat★

At the MGM Grand, 3799 Las Vegas Blvd. S. 702-891-7777. www.mgmgrand.com. Open year-round daily 11am–10pm.

MGM Grand guarantees visitors a lion's share of excitement at the hotel's new Lion Habitat. Located inside the casino next to Studio 54, the tri-story structure showcases a variety of African lions and cubs, including Goldie, Metro and Baby Lion, a direct descendant of MGM Studio's famous signature marquee lion, Metro. Besides adding an adventurous element to the hotel, the lion habitat educates guests about these magnificent creatures.

To Ride With Lions

Evans transports lions from his property, which is 12mi from the MGM Grand, to the hotel two to three times a day. Accustomed to humans, and comfortable in front of a camera, the felines are very much at home being up-close and personal with their human counterparts. There are between one and five animals in the habitat at any given period; no group stays in the structure for more than six hours at a time.

You'll see lions up, down and all around as they romp throughout the $9 million 5,345sq ft structure, which is enclosed by glass. Encased by skylights, the habitat boasts 35ft-high walls to allow visitors the opportunity to watch the lions' every move. Lions can literally encircle you at any time via a see-through walkway tunnel that runs through the habitat, allowing the animals to prowl above and below.

Veteran animal trainer/owner Keith Evans owns, oversees, trains, feeds and nurtures the animals. He also helped design the habitat. Adorned with trees and foliage, and featuring four waterfalls, overhangs and a pond, the habitat is designed to resemble the lions' natural environment.

The Secret Garden of Siegfried & Roy★

At The Mirage, 3400 Las Vegas Blvd. S. 702-791-7111 or 800-627-6667. www.themirage.com. Open May–Aug Mon, Tue, Thu & Fri 11am–5pm, weekends 10am–5pm. Rest of the year closes at 3:30pm. Closed Wed.

It's the best-kept secret in town. Lush manicured grass, graceful palm trees, bright flowers, and crystal-clear waterfalls and pools abound within the borders of this ethereal place. In the background, the calls of exotic birds and jungle drums play over loudspeakers.

Oh, you may hear a few roars now and then, but that's only the satisfied residents itching to let the cat out of the bag about this 15-acre refuge. They want to share with the public what is most cherished by world-renowned illusionists Siegfried & Roy—that some of the world's rarest animals can live in harmony with one another and with mankind in the Secret Garden at the Mirage.

Opened officially in May 1997, the Secret Garden allows the public to view the amazing results of Siegfried & Roy's longtime conservation efforts. Here you'll find more than 70 animals representing six rare species that reside in the sanctuary:

- Royal white tigers of Nevada (including three cubs born in October 2002)
- White lions
- Heterozygous Bengal tigers (possessing genes for both the tawny and white color)
- Gilda, the Asian elephant (now in her mid-50s)
- Panthers
- Snow Leopards

Catting Around

According to Roy, if you have spent your life working with animals, you feel the pain of their threatened extinction even more. He and Siegfried live together with these magnificent creatures applying three simple guidelines: kindness, respect and trust.

With only chain-link fences separating animal from human, the $13 million jungle habitat showcases these beasts in their natural environment. The cats enjoy an ample amount of space for play, as well as exercise areas. Behind the garden, unseen by the public, there's an indoor-outdoor compound the size of two football fields that includes catwalks 100ft in length for exercise purposes and an air-conditioned structure housing an animal hospital, clinic and nursery.

No wonder Roy calls the animals "kings in exile!"

Something fishy's going on in Las Vegas, thanks to the fact that some casinos have been bringing in attractions that do hold water. From beady-eyed sharks to friendly dolphins, here are some ways you can get into the swim of things.

Shark Reef★★

At Mandalay Bay, 3950 Las Vegas Blvd. S. 702-632-7777 or 877-632-7000. www.mandalaybay.com. Open year-round daily 10am–11pm. $14.95 adults, $9.95 children (ages 5-12; ages 4 & under free).

Just when you thought it was safe to go back into the casino, along comes an adventure that will grip you in the "Jaws" of excitement. Shark Reef at Mandalay Bay is not your typical aquarium. This total sensory experience takes you on a journey through an ancient temple that has been slowly claimed by the sea. You end up on the deck of a sunken ship in shark-infested waters.

Developed in consultation with the Vancouver Aquarium Marine Science Center in Vancouver, Canada, one of the world's most respected marine facilities, the 90,560sq ft Shark Reef is home to a diverse cross-section of magnificent aquatic creatures, including different species of sharks, exotic fish, stingrays, reptiles and turtles. Featuring more than 2,000 specimens, the reef holds nearly 1.6 million gallons of seawater in 14 exhibits.

Treasure Bay – Meet four different species of sharks—tiger, sandbar, lemon and nurse—along with majestic green sea turtles and a variety of fish.

Crocodile Habitat – Encounter rare golden crocodiles, a hybrid between saltwater and Siamese crocs.

Lizard Lounge – Get up close to 9ft-long monitor lizards if you dare.

Touch Pool – Discover what shark skin really feels like, examine the shell of a horseshoe crab, and learn how sea stars swim along the ocean floor.

The Atlantis Aquarium

At The Forum Shops at Caesar's Palace, 3570 Las Vegas Blvd. S. 702-893-3807. www.parkplace.com/caesars. Tours daily at 1:15pm & 5:15pm.

Never bite the hand that feeds you is the golden rule at the Atlantis Aquarium, where you can watch divers feed the fish twice daily. The backdrop to the **Lost City of Atlantis** animatronic statue show, this 50,000-gallon marine aquarium contains a variety of brightly colored tropical fish. The most notable species, however, are the sharks and the stingrays.

A Fish Story

- More than 500 individual fish representing more than 100 species inhabit the Atlantis Aquarium.
- The fish range in size from two inches to a 4ft-long nurse shark, the largest in the aquarium.

Make sure you drop by at 3:15pm or 7:15pm, when you can witness the feeding frenzy as divers enter the tank. The aquarium also offers a below-the-scenes tour of the support facilities during the week *(dive shows & tours are free of charge)*.

The Dolphin Habitat

At The Mirage, 3400 Las Vegas Blvd. S. 702-791-7111 or 800-627-6667. www.themirage.com. Open May–Aug Mon–Fri 11am–7pm, weekends 10am–7pm. Rest of the year closes at 5:30pm. $12 (children under 10 free).

Located in a tropical setting behind the Mirage, Dolphin Habitat makes a huge splash with visitors year after year. The purpose of the habitat is to provide a sanctuary for Atlantic bottlenose dolphins and to educate the public about marine mammals and their environment. Since it's also a research and breeding facility, the habitat provides valuable information about the reproduction of these animals that is sending waves of excitement throughout the scientific community. All the dolphins housed here were relocated from other marine-mammal projects.

What's So Special About The Dolphin Habitat?

- It cost $20 million to build, and it's rated as one of the top facilities of its kind in the world.
- It encompasses four connecting pools holding approximately 2.5 million gallons of water—four times larger than government regulations require.
- Pools have been designed with irregularly shaped contours to allow freedom of movement for the dolphins and to minimize sound reverberation.

From the pool scene (don't miss the great summer hotel pool events) to gondolas to beaches with real sand, Las Vegas is getting more wet and wild every day. Here are some great ways to keep cool, or simply to be cool.

Mandalay Bay Lagoon

At Mandalay Bay, 3950 Las Vegas Blvd. S. 702-632-7777 or 877-632-7000. www.mandalaybay.com.

Who ever thought you could go up a lazy river in Las Vegas? Or spend a day at the beach on the Strip? If you're a guest at Mandalay Bay, you can do both. Named in the press as one of the "sexiest" hotel pools, the 11-acre Mandalay Bay tropical water environment features a sand-and-surf beach, a lazy river, three swimming pools and a jogging track.

Try floating down the **Lazy River Ride** for three-quarters of a mile on a large innertube. They don't call it "lazy" for nothing—you'll go at a relaxing snail's pace of two miles per hour. Or if you *really* want to relax, reserve a private bungalow or cabana for the day; they come equipped with snacks, drinks, a television and even a pool attendant. Conveniently located on Mandalay Beach, the Temple Bar serves tropical drinks and a healthy selection of fresh fruits and vegetables, chips and salsa, and sushi.

Beach Ball

You don't have to be a hotel guest to enjoy the Mandalay Beach Summer Concert Series that the resort presents each year. For the price of a ticket, you can lie on a towel on the sand, dip your toes in the water, and watch big-name groups (Beach Boys, Chris Isaak, Toto) perform outdoors at the beach.

What About The Beach?

- It has more than 1,700 tons of sand, brought in from Southern California so you feel that you really are on a tropical island.
- The wave pool is filled with more than 1.6 million gallons of water—and there are real waves, which can break at up to 5ft high.
- Giant flame pots on the beach shoot fire 15–20ft into the air.

The Gondolas at Lake Las Vegas

220 Grand Mediterra, Henderson, NV. From the Strip, take Las Vegas Blvd. South to Tropicana Ave. Take US-95 South to exit for Lake Mead Dr. Go left (east) on Lake Mead Dr. to Lake Las Vegas Pkwy. 877-446-6365. www.gondola.com or www.lakelasvegas.com.

They may not exactly be the *Nina*, the *Pinta* and the *Santa Maria*, but the *Serenissima* and *La Fenice* are breaking new ground—and new waters—at the posh Lake Las Vegas Resort, 17mi from the Las Vegas Strip. In keeping with the resort's Mediterranean theme, the *Serenissima* and *La Fenice* are gondolas that take visitors for a romantic ride and offer them dinner and other culinary delights at the same time.

Cruises To Choose From:

Classic Cruise – This one-hour cruise comes complete with Godiva chocolates and champagne *($125/2 passengers)*.

Basket Lunch Cruise – Spend an hour one afternoon on the water and have a picnic lunch, including beverages *($145/2 passengers)*.

Destination Dinner Cruise – Cruise to the Lake Las Vegas Resort restaurant of your choice and sip champagne along the way. It takes an hour to cruise to the resort, as well as an hour and a half for dinner *($175/2 passengers, not including dinner)*.

Gourmet Dinner Cruise – During this one-and-a-half-hour excursion you'll dine in style on a three-course catered gourmet meal served on fine china, crystal and silver *($255/2 passengers)*.

Go Jump in a Lake

Situated on a privately owned, 320-acre lake, Lake Las Vegas Resort is a premier residential and resort destination that has been honored internationally as one of ten significant new projects that will define urban life in the 21C. The 2,600-acre master-planned resort offers residential housing (Celine Dion lives here), world-class resort hotels (the Hyatt Regency and the Ritz Carlton), a collection of six signature golf courses, a casino, shopping and spas.

When it comes to attractions to impress Las Vegas' visitors, the sky's the limit. You'll find it easy to have your head in the clouds when you experience Vegas' highest pleasures.

The Eiffel Tower★★

At Paris Las Vegas, 3655 Las Vegas Blvd. S. 702-946-7000 or 800-634-3434. www.parislv.com.

This is one attraction that has literally gone through the roof, and hovers 50 stories over the Las Vegas Strip. The 540ft-tall Eiffel Tower at Paris Las Vegas, the hotel's centerpiece and signature landmark, is an exact half-replica of the one in Paris, France. Three of the tower's four gigantic legs spring from the resort's 85,000sq ft casino floor and rise through its ceiling. This is a heavy-duty Vegas must-see—it weighs in at more than 7 million pounds.

Construction of the tower replica and of other authentic re-creations here—the Arc de Triomphe, the Paris Opera House and the Louvre—began with research. A team of architects, designers and hotel executives made numerous trips to Paris to photograph and sketch the famous landmarks to capture the intricate details that make each one unique. Designers obtained Gustav Eiffel's original 1889 drawings to help execute the massive undertaking. Construction was challenging, to say the least, especially in light of the fact that there are major differences in climate and wind velocity between the "City of Lights" (Paris) and the "Neon Jungle" (Vegas). Not to mention modern-day building and fire codes.

Unlike the French original, Paris Las Vegas' Eiffel Tower is fireproof and stable enough to withstand earthquakes. It is also welded together rather than riveted like the original, although the designers painstakingly added the rivets to ensure the authenticity of the tower's appearance. The lighting system was designed to the exact specifications of the lighting that was added to the real Eiffel Tower for its 100th anniversary in 1989.

The Eiffel Tower Restaurant

See the glittering city of Las Vegas at night from the 11th-story Eiffel Tower Restaurant. Here in the softly lit dining room with its romantic piano bar, you'll savor classic French fare. And the waitstaff is fluent in both English and French.

The Stratosphere Tower★

2000 Las Vegas Blvd. S. 702-380-7777 or 800-998-6937. www.strat.lv.com.

The tallest free-standing structure west of the Mississippi, the Stratosphere Tower soars to a height of 1,149ft (135 stories tall). It's taller than the Seattle Space Needle, the Tokyo Tower and the Eiffel Tower (the real one) and forever changed the skyline of Las Vegas when it was completed in November 1995.

A gourmet restaurant, meeting facilities, two thrill rides and two observation decks—an indoor and an outdoor deck—occupy the tower's 12 uppermost levels. Also known as the "pod," these upper stories rest upon the tower's three "legs." One of four double-decker elevators traveling at 1,800 feet per minute will whisk you up to the pod. To travel from the ground level to the pod takes less than 30 seconds.

From the indoor observation deck, take the elevators to the world's highest thrill rides, the Big Shot and the High Roller *(see Must Ride).*

The Top of the World Restaurant

You'll be sitting on top of the world when you sit down to eat at the Stratosphere Tower's gourmet restaurant, 800ft in the air. Located on the 106th floor, the room revolves 360 degrees in one hour, giving you unparalleled **views**★★ of all sides of the city.

Open for lunch and dinner seven days a week, the restaurant serves an eclectic menu including fresh seafood, steaks and pasta. One level up from the restaurant, the Top of the World Lounge features a wide selection of cigars, wines, beers and spirits, as well as live entertainment.

Where else but Vegas can you find renowned designers, celebrity chefs, nightclubs and ultra-lounges co-existing peacefully alongside Blue Men and Trekkies? Some attractions are just light years away from the rest.

Blue Man Group

At Luxor, 3900 Las Vegas Blvd. S. 702-262-4900 or 800-557-7428. www.luxor.com.

Can a group of three blue men acting as one entity make its descent upon Las Vegas and carry audiences off to a new realm where art and science intersect? Will UFOs, in the form of gumballs, marshmallows and other food objects that fly from mouths onto canvases, along with spurting fountains of paint, forever become part of the everyday landscape of Vegas entertainment?

For the answer to these questions, take in the saga of "the bald and the blue-tiful," otherwise known as Blue Man Group Live at Luxor, a performance troupe with bald, cobalt-blue heads (thanks to grease paint). The group is playing in the Luxor Theatre for an indefinite run.

It's hard to explain why anyone would want to clean up the biggest mess this side of the Sierra Nevada that Blue Man Group leaves on the stage after their show. During their act, the blue men neither talk nor show emotion. They express themselves through art and music, and the result only goes to prove that whatever has been living inside of them all these years definitely needs to get out.

It's a Blue World

Chris Wink, who along with Matt Goldman and Phil Stanton created Blue Man Group, describes their work as "Techno-tribal." In one segment, they pour paint into a drum with a light inside it, and the drum explodes 25ft into the air like a rocket. They then put a canvas over it and make a painting they call "abstract expression-ism." For people who know art, there are a lot of inside jokes hidden in this act, which the group refers to as "art-world science."

Star Trek: The Experience

At the Las Vegas Hilton, 3000 Paradise Rd. 702-732-5111 or 800-732-7117. www.parkplace.com. Open daily 11am–11pm. $24.99 for an all-day pass.

If you want to go where no casino attraction has gone before—into the 21st century—then Star Trek: The Experience at the Las Vegas Hilton is the only way to fly. Personalized entertainment at its futuristic best, the journey begins when you are beamed aboard an exact replica of the starship USS *Enterprise*, where you will meet the crew members. After receiving your mission, you take the Turbo-Lift to the Grand Corridor, a never-before-seen area in the world of Star Trek, where you are escorted to the Shuttle Bay. Here you board a 27-seat shuttlecraft for the ultimate simulator journey through the Star Trek universe—the trick is to get back home.

Those who experience motion sickness can skip the ride and head straight for Quark's Bar and Restaurant. There you can enjoy all sorts of drinks and gastronomical delights such as Little Green Salads, Power Grid Potstickers, Flaming Ribs of Targ, Hamborger, Glop on a Stick, Final Frontier Desserts and much more.

History of the Future Museum – Houses the largest collection of Star Trek props, costumes and memorabilia in the world, with more than 200 items.

Fly-Buy

If a shopping trip is in order, visit the **Deep Space Nine Promenade**, stocked with an unusual collection of authentic prop pieces from Paramount Pictures, expertly crafted pewter and cold-cast resin model ships, artwork and collectibles. **Garak's Clothes Exchange** offers apparel for the entire family, including men's and women's replicas of Star Trek uniforms.

Moogie's Trading Post sells everything from glassware to sweets and teas. Many of the pieces at **Latinum Jewelers** incorporate the Star Trek logo. **Zek's Grand Emporium** contains more Star Trek merchandise—key chains, plush toys, posters, books and calendars.

If all that doesn't satiate your appetite for adventure, you can gamble inside Star Trek: The Experience, too!

L et Las Vegas take you for a ride. Your fun factor will go from 0 to 60 miles per hour in an instant when you experience some of the thrill attractions in the city.

The Big Shot

At the Stratosphere Tower, Level 112. 2000 Las Vegas Blvd. S. 702-380-7777 or 800-998-6937. www.stratlv.com. Riders must be at least 48 inches tall. $13.

If you're looking for a shot of adrenaline, treat yourself to the Big Shot, one of the world's two highest thrill rides. Recently named by Forbes FYI Magazine as the "Best Adrenaline Rush," Big Shot is only for the truly daring.

The ride carries a total of 12 passengers at a time, launching them 160ft in 2.5 seconds up the 238ft mast that extends like a needle from the top of the Tower. You'll experience four Gs of pressure on the way up. They you'll hang suspended for a split second before hitting zero-G weightlessness on the way down as you fall faster than a free fall, reaching speeds of up to 45mph. If your eyes aren't closed, you'll get a great view of the city.

The High Roller

At the Stratosphere Tower, Level 112. 2000 Las Vegas Blvd. S. 702-380-7777 or 800-998-6937. www.stratlv.com. Riders must be at least 48 inches tall. $11.

By now you've probably guessed that the second of the world's two highest rides is also at the Stratosphere. This one gives a whole new definition to the term High Roller, as it circles around the outer edge of the Stratosphere Tower on 865ft of track. The big bet here is that if you don't have a cast-iron stomach, you'll be rolling in a different way. Seating a total of 28 riders in seven four-passenger cars, the coaster makes six clockwise motions, banking sharply at 32 degrees and reaching speeds of up to 30 miles per hour. A word of advice: Don't eat right before going on either of these rides.

In Search of the Obelisk

At Luxor, 3900 Las Vegas Blvd. S. 702-262-4000 or 800-288-1000. www.luxor.com. $7.

For action-packed indoor fun, try some pyramid power. This IMAX Ridefilm takes you on a journey as mystical as the Egyptian pyramids. The story line begins in April 1992, back when Luxor was under construction. A spectacular subterranean civilization is discovered beneath the pyramid. You board a levitating vehicle to go in search of the "Obelisk," a mysterious crystal object, and are whisked away to an archaeological dig site to inspect the findings firsthand. With evil forces lurking throughout the temple, the action adventure, with all its twists and turns, soon elevates into a high-speed chase, leading you into vast cavernous areas and parts unknown. Look out Indiana Jones!

Manhattan Express Roller Coaster

At New York-New York, 3790 Las Vegas Blvd. S. 702-740-6969 or 888-693-6763. www.nynyhotelcasino.com. $12.

Around and around and around she goes, when she stops, you'll definitely know. Just try to smile at the end of your Manhattan Express roller coaster ride (even if you're feeling pretty green). That's when the pictures are taken.

The Manhattan Express twists, loops and dives at speeds up to 60 miles per hour as the roller coaster winds around skyscrapers and Miss Liberty. At times, your whole world will literally turn upside down. This ride features the first-ever "heartline" twist and dive maneuver, which creates the sensation that a pilot feels when going through a barrel role in an airplane. In this portion of the ride, the train rolls 180 degrees, suspending its riders 86ft above the casino roof before diving directly under itself—hold on to your hats!

Who says you can't get something for nothing? Some of the best things in life are free in Las Vegas, too. That includes the pleasures derived from the city's many physical attractions—even if they are of the nonhuman variety.

Bellagio Fountains★★

At Bellagio (see Casinos), 3600 Las Vegas Blvd. S. 702-693-7111 or 888-987-6667. www.bellagioresort.com

The Fountains of Bellagio are undoubtedly the big shot of the Strip. Twice an hour (every 15 minutes at night) the 1,100 fountains shoot as high as 240ft into the air, choreographed to music ranging from the classic arias of Luciano Pavarotti to show tunes to Lionel Ritchie to the romantic stylings of Frank Sinatra. More than a thousand fountains dance in front of the hotel, At just barely under 20 million gallons and approximately 8.5 acres, Lake Bellagio is the largest musical fountain system in the world.

Bellagio Conservatory and Botanical Gardens★

Just beyond the lobby at Bellagio is the lovely conservatory garden with its 50ft-high glass ceiling. The ceiling framework and beams are sculpted in floral patterns from oxidized copper, called verde.

With the change of each season, the garden puts on a different face, with new trees and flowers. It also puts on spectacular displays for Thanksgiving, Christmas and the Chinese New Year.

Fremont Street Experience★★

425 Fremont St. 702-678-5777. www.vegasexperience.com.

If you're traveling downtown from the Strip, it may feel like Las Vegas has disappeared somewhere between St. Louis Avenue and Fremont Street. Don't give up, just keep on going and you'll definitely see the light. Or lights, that is—over two million light bulbs to be exact.

Since it opened in December 1995, the Fremont Street Experience has turned up the wattage in downtown Las Vegas every night with a spectacular computer-generated sound-and-light show. The Experience is a modern tech-nological and engineering marvel, the only one of its kind in the world.

Suspended 90ft over downtown, a four-acre barrel-arched canopy jolts to life several times nightly above a four-block section of Fremont Street *(between Main & 4th Sts.)*. Holding it aloft are 16 columns, each weighing 26,000 pounds and each capable of bearing 400,000 pounds.

The illuminated extravaganza of flashing, rolling images is generated by more than 2 million fiber-optic lights and synchronized to music from a 540,000-watt sound system. Created by a consortium of 11 casinos, the attraction has transformed downtown's five-block principal thoroughfare into a mix of urban theater, sound-and-light shows, and a variety of dining, entertainment and shopping venues. Under its high dome, the canopy creates a pedestrian mall closed to traffic and encompassing several of Las Vegas' most popular down-town casinos, including the Golden Nugget.

"Watts" Up On Fremont Street?

- 180 computer-programmed, high-intensity strobe lights

- 64 variable-color lighting fixtures that can produce 300 colors

- 8 robotic mirrors per block that can be individually programmed to pan and tilt to reflect light

Mirage Volcano★

At The Mirage, 3400 Las Vegas Blvd. S. 702-791-7111 or 800-627-6667. www.themirage.com.

There's going to be a rumble on the Las Vegas Strip tonight—only this one will be coming from a volcano.

Each evening, at the main entrance to the Mirage, facing the Strip, a rumbling sound begins, fog appears, and the volcano shoots smoke and fire 100ft above the lagoon that lies at its base. Spewing fire every 15 minutes from sunset until midnight, the volcano erupts about 14 times a day in the summer and about 23 times a day in the winter. Each display lasts about two minutes. (Volcano shows don't take place if it's too windy.)

Set off by a computer program that basically runs itself, the fiberglass volcano's operation is overseen by three main crew members each night. There are 34 special effects connected with the volcano, which take place thanks to natural gas lines running in the front and sides of the lagoon. The natural gas produces real flames in the water, much like igniting your oven at home. They work in conjunction with the lights to give the volcano its erupting effect.

The Sirens of Treasure Island★

At Treasure Island, 3300 Las Vegas Blvd. S. 702-894-7111 or 800-944-7444. www.treasureislandlasvegas.com.

Since its inception, the **The Pirate Battle of Buccaneer Bay at Treasure Island**★★ was always what the name implied, a 12-minute fight to the finish between a British frigate, the HMS *Britannia*, and a pirate ship, the *Hispaniola*.

In tandem with the hotel's 10th anniversary, in October 2003, a new show called The Sirens of TI was unveiled. A sensual, modern interpretation of the Pirate Battle, male pirates are now joined by female sirens, who are part muse, part seductress and part pirate. Directed and choreographed by Kenny Ortega (of *Dirty Dancing* fame), the new show is a modern pop musical stage show with singing, dancing, feats of amazing strength, pyrotechnics and sound. Ortega claims that the sirens are his inspiration for the storyline.

Air Play

At the Tropicana, 3801 Las Vegas Blvd. S. 702-739-2222 or 800-634-4000.
www.tropicanalv.com.

You don't have to look far to discover what's up lately at the Tropicana. The hotel's newest creative venture, Air Play, takes place in and above the casino, giving an entirely new meaning to the term glass ceiling.

Free to the public, this 20-minute dynamic display of music, dancing and acrobatics takes place four times a day, seven days a week, on a stage set amid slot machines below the hotel's historic Tiffany-designed **stained-glass ceiling**. With high-flying performers, jugglers, contortionists and other unique acts, Air Play certainly adds to the casino action.

The featured act in Air Play is called Aerial Expression and stars Chris Santistevan and Jon Harms. In their 20-minute one-of-a-kind act, the two men "fly" from straps that are connected by a rail system (a travel track), which, in turn, is controlled by a computer. The rail is attached to the Tiffany stained-glass ceiling, allowing the adagio team to glide up and down and travel 100ft across the length of the casino floor.

The Festival of Fountains

At The Forum Shops at Caesars Palace, 3570 Las Vegas Blvd. S. 702-893-4800.
www.simon.com.

When visitors see the Festival of Fountains at the Forum Shops at Caesars Palace, heads will turn and tongues will wag, and that's just what the statues will be doing, too. You can't help but be amazed at the new level of animatronics reached in this attraction.

The party starts when Bacchus, the god of wine and merriment, wakes up and decides to throw a fete for himself and Forum visitors. He enlists the powers of Apollo, the god of music; Venus, the goddess of love; and Plutus, the god of wealth. As the festivities begin, the statues talk and move, enhanced by special effects such as lasers and lighting.

The entire show, from animation to sound, water and lighting effects, is controlled by computer. Each statue's voice is a scripted recording that runs on a cue list that "talks" to the computer. There are over 700 cues for one entire show, which lasts about eight minutes.

Masquerade Show in the Sky

At the Rio, 3700 W. Flamingo Rd. 702-777-7777 or 800-752-9746. www.playrio.com.

BevErtainment

Rio guests have the opportunity to drink in an energetic new casino experience that is ensuring that casino beverage service will never be the same. The hotel recently introduced BevErtainment, a new concept that marries cocktail service with entertainment. Nearly 100 glamorous and talented female and male entertainers criss-cross the casino floor, not only taking drink orders but stopping periodically to grace strategically placed stages for 90-second performances. Some sing, some dance, and all bring your drinks quickly and with a smile.

You don't have to buy a drink to watch the action. There are 10 stages, or "hot spots," throughout the Rio's casino floor. When the lights begin to flash and you hear the strains of a musical introduction, you know you're in for a treat. All the BevErtainers are professional singers or dancers and perform approximately nine solo numbers during an eight-hour serving shift.

Things are definitely looking up at the Rio. The property offers the spectacular Masquerade Show in the Sky, a $25-million interactive entertainment experience in the spirit of Brazil's Carnavale. The show consists of five complete parades—Village Street Party, South of the Border, Carnivale, Venice Masquerade and New Orleans Mardi Gras—that alternate throughout the day. Each 12-minute show comes with different music, costumes and live performances by the 26-member cast.

Five performer-filled floats, each boasting its own individually themed music and sound system, move on a 950ft track 13ft above the casino floor of Masquerade Village. You can join in the fun from viewing vantage points on the first and second floors of the village. Or, for a small fee, you can cavort with the entertainers by dressing in costume and climbing aboard one of the floats. There is a catch—and hopefully it's yours as the entertainers throw out bright strands of beads from the floats to the crowds below.

The Thunderstorm at the Desert Passage

At the Aladdin, 3667 Las Vegas Blvd. S. 702-866-0703 or 888-800-8284.
www.desertpassage.com.

You'll definitely let a smile be your umbrella with this attraction at the Desert Passage shopping area at the Aladdin. The sound of waves lapping onto shore in the distance will draw you towards Merchants Harbor, a breathtaking replica of a North African harborfront. Here you'll discover the hull of a 155ft-long European steamer moored in port. Sounds of footsteps along the wooden gangway echo through the streets as longshoremen scramble to unload new merchandise for trading. Scattered clouds drift across the sky, fog rolls in, the breeze builds, far-off thunder rumbles and a gentle rain falls. The four-minute show goes off at various intervals, run by a computer program that coordinates all the special effects. Fog is produced by fog misters on the 80ft-tall ship, while five wind generators—large fans that are hidden around the harbor area—provide the wind. Lights are dimmed to simulate the darkening sky.

Behind The Scenes

The sounds of thunder and wind are actual recordings of the real things; strobe lights create flashes of lightning. As for the rain, 32 quarter-inch spray nozzles in the ceiling have specialized valves that disperse the water laterally to create rain droplets. Pumps activate nozzles and a series of computer-programmed valves to regulate the levels of rain from a light drizzle to a downpour.

The Tropicana Bird Show starring Tiana Carroll

At the Tropicana, 3801 Las Vegas Blvd. S. 702-739-2222 or 800-634-4000.
www.tropicanalv.com.

Here's an afternoon show in Vegas that's definitely for the birds. The Tropicana Bird Show, which takes place in the hotel's Tropics Lounge three times daily, displays all the talent that Tiana Carroll has under her wing. You'll meet Mariah, the funny fowl (or class clown, as the case may be), who follows Carroll around in the 20-minute show. Then there's Mango, a Moluccan cockatoo that talks, rides a bird-size motorbike and skates on roller blades. Dorothy, a yellow-nape Amazon, sings a duet, "How Much Is That Doggie in the Window?," with Meko, a Congo-African grey parrot. Audiences are encouraged to cheer on the winged creatures during the party section of the show. The loudest person gets to have a picture taken with Carroll and Mariah.

Leaving Las Vegas for a day trip into its scenic environs can provide more than just a getaway from the action of the city. It can offer a quiet foray into some of the most interesting geological formations of the Old West.

Red Rock Canyon★★

17mi west of Las Vegas via W. Charleston Blvd. (Rte. 159). Look for sign on right to Red Rock Scenic Drive. Red Rock Visitors Center is located at 1000 Scenic Dr. 702-363-1921. www.redrockcanyon.blm.gov. Hours vary depending on season. $5/car.

A 20-minute drive from the Las Vegas Strip, the towering sandstone bluffs of Red Rock Canyon are magnificent to a fault—the Keystone Thrust Fault, the most significant geologic feature of the canyon. Scientists think that some 65 million years ago, two of the earth's crustal plates collided with such force that part of one plate was shoved up and over younger sandstone through this fracture in the earth's crust. This thrust is clearly defined by the sharp contrast between the gray limestone and red sandstone formations.

The centerpiece of the canyon is a stunning sheer escarpment of banded red, white and gray rock, more than 13mi long and almost 3,000ft high. Formed from sand dunes cemented and tinted by water acting on iron oxide and calcium carbonate, the escarpment represents the western part of the Navajo Sandstone Formation in the Colorado Plateau.

With more than 30mi of trails, the 300sq mi **Red Rock Canyon National Conservation Area**★★ preserves the northern end of the formation. The area's **Red Rock Visitors Center**★ is the place to get all the info you need. A recorded tour takes you through the geologic and wildlife history of the area.

Rock Steady

From the visitors center, you can drive the 13mi **Scenic Loop**. Open to traffic from 7am to dusk, the drive features several vista points that offer panoramic views of spectacular rock formations. Highlights along the Loop Road include:

- **Sandstone Quarry**★★, where rock was mined in the early 20C.
- **Willow Spring** with its ancient petroglyphs.
- **Ice-Box Canyon Trail**★, a 2.5mi hike into a steep, narrow canyon.

Valley of Fire State Park★★

55mi northeast of Las Vegas via I-15 North to Hwy. 169. Visitor Center is located on Rte. 169 in Overton, NV. 702-397-2088. http://parks.nv.gov/vf.htm. Open year-round daily 8:30am–dusk. $5.

You may think you're on Mars when you first gaze upon the jagged limestone mounds of fiery scarlet, vermilion and mauve that rise out of the stark Mojave Desert. The 56,000-acre park, which was dedicated in 1935 as Nevada's first state park, takes its name from its distinctive coloration. The red sandstone formations that make up this surreal scene were formed from great sand dunes during the Jurassic Period. Complex uplifting and faulting in the region, followed by 100 million years of erosion, have carved this 6mi-long and 4mi-wide crimson-hued valley from the desert. In the process, water and wind have shaped the land into arches, domes, spires and serrated ridges.

Valley of Fire is famous for its **petroglyphs**, ancient rock art left behind by the prehistoric Basketmaker people and the Anasazi Pueblo farmers who lived along the Muddy River between 300 BC and AD 1150.

It's wise to stop at the visitor center before exploring the area. There you can pick up maps, trail guides and books, and learn about the ecology, geology and history of the region. There's also a desert tortoise habitat where you can see the endangered animals at close range. The driving tour through the valley takes about 15–20 minutes, longer if you take time to get out of the car to see some of the fascinating sights along the way.

Self-Guided Driving Tour Highlights

Mouse's Tank★★ – The intriguing **Petroglyph Canyon Trail★★** *(.8mi)* crosses a narrow canyon to Mouse's Tank. Named for a Paiute Indian who hid from the law here in 1897, this natural rock basin collects rainwater and provides a watering spot for birds, reptiles, mammals and insects.

White Domes Area★★ – From the visitor center, a 7mi spur road leads to the White Domes, a landscape of mulitcolored monuments and smooth, wind-carved sandstone.

Atlatl Rock★ – On the west end of the park, a steep metal stairway climbs up to Atlatl Rock, where you'll find a rare petroglyph of an atlatl, a notched stick used to throw primitive spears.

Natural Sites

Mojave National Preserve★

53mi south of Las Vegas via I-15, in Baker, CA; or 113mi south of Furnace Creek via I-15 to Rte. 127. Baker Desert Information Center, 72157 Baker Blvd., Baker, CA (760-733-4040; open year-round daily 9am–5pm); Needles Desert Information Center, 707 W. Broadway, Needles, CA (760-326-6322; open year-round Tue–Sun 8am–4pm). www.nps.gov/moja.

If you're wondering just how vast and empty the desert can be, the Mojave National Preserve is the answer to your question. An easy day trip from Las Vegas, the 1.6 million-acre preserve (which begins near Baker, California) is crisscrossed by both paved and dirt roads. The Mojave is home to nearly 300 species of animals and some 700 species of plants, including the nation's largest forest of Joshua trees.

The 2,500sq mi wedge-shaped preserve encompasses a landscape of lava mesas, precipitous mountain ranges, sand dunes, limestone caverns, dry lake beds and lava tubes. Although mines and ranches still operate in the area—pay attention to "No Trespassing" signs—evidence of human habitation is rare. Livestock graze under a provision of the California Desert Protection Act and hunting is allowed, even though half the preserve is designated as wilderness.

Tips for Visiting

The best time to visit is in spring or autumn. Temperatures between mid-May and mid-September soar upwards from 100°F.

The 67mi circuit from Baker via Kelbaker Road, Kelso-Cima Road and Cima Road to I-15 is a good introduction to the preserve's sights.

Don't Miss These Highlights:

Hole-in-the-Wall★★ – This jumble of volcanic cliffs, one of the more bizarre geologic features of Black Canyon, is profusely pocked with clefts and cavities.

Kelso Dunes★ – These 45 acres of sand dunes are among the highest in the Mojave (600ft above the desert floor).

Mitchell Caverns★ – Six limestone caverns are concealed within the Providence Mountains that were formed by percolating groundwater millions of years ago.

Spring Mountains National Recreation Area ★

35mi northwest of downtown Las Vegas. From the Strip, take I-15 West to Hwy. 95 North. Stay on Hwy. 95 until you get to Kyle Canyon Rd. and follow signs for Mt. Charleston. 702-515-5400. www.fs.fed.us.htnf. Call the US Forest Service (702-673-8800) for campground information. Open daily 8am–dusk. $5.

If you're pining for a beautiful alpine wilderness spot to get away from it all, Mt. Charleston and the surrounding Toiyabe National Forest is a popular destination for hiking, backpacking, picnicking and overnight camping. Thick bristlecone pines (among the oldest trees on earth) clinging to the limestone cliffs 10,000ft above the desert floor make an awesome backdrop for whatever your pleasure may be.

The fifth-highest mountain in the state, at just under 12,000ft, Mt. Charleston experiences temperatures that are usually anywhere from 20 to 40 degrees cooler than the city, rarely going above 80 degrees in the summer. You'll notice the change in vegetation at each increment as the elevation increases. Besides the distinctive plant life, many animals inhabit the Mt. Charleston area. Among them is the Palmer chipmunk, which is found nowhere else in the world. The region is also home to bighorn sheep, elk, coyotes, bobcats, foxes and cougars.

The US Forest Service maintains more than 50mi of marked hiking trails for all abilities at Mt. Charleston. Trails range from .25mi long to the strenuous 8.3mi **South Loop Trail**, which climbs to the mountain's summit at 11,918ft from the head of Kyle Canyon Road.

When You're Not Roughing It

For those who prefer civilization, the **Mt. Charleston Hotel** *(2 Kyle Canyon Rd.; 702-872-5500)* at an elevation slightly below the timberline, has a mountain lodge atmosphere with fantastic views.

The only other place for provisions is the **Mt. Charleston Lodge** *(702-872-5408)*, a popular restaurant and bar at the end of Kyle Canyon Road. If you want to escape the Strip, rent one of the log cabins, which are equipped with two-person whirlpool tubs, fireplaces and private decks.

While much of Las Vegas doesn't kid around, there are a handful of attractions and shows in the city that focus on child's play. This is Vegas family fun at its best.

The Adventuredome

At Circus Circus,
2880 Las Vegas Blvd. S.
702-734-0410 or
800-634-3450.
www.circuscircus-lasvegas.com.
Open year-round daily 10am–
midnight. $3–5 per ride; $19.95
all-day pass.

America's largest indoor theme park, the Adventuredome features the world's only indoor double-loop, double-corkscrew roller coaster—the **Canyon Blaster**—which reaches a top speed of 55mph. Set in a Grand Canyon motif, the theme park goes out of its way to ensure that visitors get their "piece of the rock" when it comes to entertainment, packing 19 attractions under its glass-domed five acres. Since opening its doors in August 1993 with four rides, the Adventuredome has welcomed in excess of 15 million visitors.

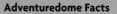

Adventuredome Facts

- Adventuredome is 200ft high.
- It is fully enclosed by 8,615 panes of glass, each weighing in at over 300 pounds.
- Adventuredome took a year to build and cost $90 million.

Besides the Canyon Blaster, other top attractions include the **Rim Runner** boat ride, which climaxes in a 60ft water plunge and **Fun House Express**. **Chaos** whirls riders in all three dimensions of motion, and the **Inverter** turns

riders upside down. Team-laser-tag enthusiasts will want to head for **Lazer Blast**. Adventurers of all ages flock to the **Extreme Zone** to climb walls, bounce into air on a "bungee trampoline" or try their skill at Pike's Pass, an 18-hole miniature golf course.

If high-tech motion-simulator rides are your thing, then the Adventuredome's new **IMAX Ridefilm Cineplex** is for you. IMAX ReBoot: The Ride, which will take you on a warp-speed journey through cyberspace, is the first movie ride produced for the IMAX Ridefilm system using all computer-generated images.

Babes in Adventureland

The Adventuredome has many attractions suitable for younger children, including the traditional carousel, a roller coaster (Miner Mike) and Cliffhangers, a playspace with crawl-through tunnels, slides and more. The park offers bumper cars, carnival-style games, clown shows, arcade games and a snack bar.

Everything Coca-Cola Las Vegas

Showcase Mall. 702-270-5965 or 702-597-3122. www.vegas.com/shopping/showcase.htm. Open Mon–Sun 10am–11pm.

If you want to keep the kids content, show them the bottle—the 100ft-tall Coca-Cola bottle on the Strip that is the trademark of Everything Coca-Cola. On two floors here you'll find everything you can imagine that has to do with the soft-drink brand. A soda fountain on the second floor offers ice-cream floats and other concoctions, all made with Coca-Cola products. Retail items range from a $1 souvenir to collectibles that go as high as $2,500 (for one-of-a-kind items such as memorabilia from Coca-Cola-sponsored NASCAR events).

Gameworks

Showcase Mall, 3785 Las Vegas Blvd. S. 702-432-4263 or 702-597-3122. www.vegas.com/shopping/showcase.htm. Open year-round Sun–Thu 8am–midnight, Fri & Sat 10am–2am.

A unique high-tech entertainment destination where you can eat, drink, party and experience state-of-the-art interactive attractions, Gameworks knows how to push the fun button for each member of the family. Here you'll find more than 200 of the newest games, many designed exclusively for Gameworks, as well as old-fashioned pinball machines. These include multisensory games based on the movies *Star Wars* and *Jurassic Park*, as well as Indy 500, Ford Racing Zone, and VR2002 Roller Coaster. There's even a five-story climbing wall. Gameworks also features a high-energy bar area (a good place for parents to take a break) and a full-service restaurant.

M&M's World Las Vegas

At Showcase Mall, 3785 Las Vegas Blvd. S. 702-736-7611 or 702-597-3122. www.vegas.com/shopping/showcase.htm. Open year-round Sun–Thu 9am–11pm, Fri & Sat 9am–midnight.

The sweet taste of success awaits you at M&M's World in the form of a four-story monument to chocolate. An interactive shopping and retail complex, each floor of this chocolate-lover's dream offers a different layer of M&M's brand merchandise items, which number in the thousands.

You won't want to miss the M&M's Racing Team Shop; Colorworks, where you can sample 21 different colors of plain and peanut M&M's; and Ethel M Chocolates, the ultimate gourmet chocolate boutique. And it all melts in your mouth, not in your hands at the fourth-floor ice cream/candy shop. *I Lost My M In Vegas*, a complimentary 3-D movie attraction, plays seven days a week on the third floor. Kids who choose to "enroll" at M&M Academy can take part in the movie.

Tournament of Kings

At Excalibur. 3850 Las Vegas Blvd. S. 702-597-7777 or 800-937-7777. www.excalibur-casino.com. Shows nightly 6:30pm & 8:30pm. $41.95, dinner included.

When was the last time you told your kids that it was okay for them to eat with their hands? At the Tournment of Kings at Excalibur, it's the order of the day. A finger-licking good meal goes hand-in-hand with a genuine jousting tournament and great special effects, including dragons and fire wizards, that make this show a royal treat for the entire family.

The story begins when King Arthur gathers his fellow kings of Europe for a no-holds-barred competition to honor his son. Rival kings begin the games, riding their faithful steeds through round after round of medieval sport, testing their agility, strength and endurance.

As the event winds down and the victorious king takes his celebration lap, the evil wizard, Mordred, attacks, dampening the festivities and threatening to throw the world of Avalon into an age of fire and shadows. Kingdoms clash, beasts attack and fire burns bright. Arthur is mortally wounded, but before he dies, he asks his son (the show takes some artistic license with the original tale) to avenge his death.

You're Jousting!

In the Tournament of Kings, audience participation is an integral part of the fun. Each of the seven kings wears a different color (representing seven different countries) and the Dragon Knight wears black. The crowd is seated in eight different sections, corresponding to a particular king and his color (or to the Dragon Knight). Sections cheer their king on, and from show to show, no one knows which one will win.

Medieval Village

If you trade in your horse for a ride on a tall escalator, you'll find yourself on Excalibur's second floor walking straight into a fairytale medieval Village. Wonderful shops (some offering medieval-style merchandise), restaurants (including a delicious buffet), and costumed strolling singers, musicians and jugglers add to the lively atmosphere. In the middle of it all, a stage area offers free shows, including puppetry, music, storytelling and juggling.

More Kids' Stuff

The Lion Habitat ★

*At the MGM Grand, 3799 Las Vegas
Blvd. S. 702-891-7777.
www.mgmgrand.com.
Open year-round daily 11am–10pm.*

Las Vegas may not have a zoo,
but it certainly has its share
of lions. The three-story Lion
Habitat at MGM Grand houses
a variety of African lions and
cubs, including Goldie, Metro
and Baby Lion. You'll see the
big cats from all angles in
the glass-enclosed 5,345sq ft
structure, as you walk through
the see-through tunnel that runs
through the habitat.

The Secret Garden of Siegfried & Roy ★

*At The Mirage, 3400 Las Vegas Blvd. 702-791-7111 or 800-627-6667. www.themirage.com.
Open May–Aug Mon, Tue, Thu & Fri 11am–5pm, weekends 10am–5pm. Rest of the year
closes at 3:30pm. Closed Wed. $12 (children under 10 free).*

You'll think you're in the jungle when you enter this lush 15-acre refuge, complete with palm trees, flowers, waterfalls and the calls of exotic birds and
jungle drums playing in the background. Here you'll find Royal white tigers
(kids will love the three adorable cubs born in October 2002), white lions,
Bengal tigers, snow leopards, an Asian elephant and more.

The Dolphin Habitat

*At The Mirage, 3400 Las Vegas Blvd. S. 702-791-7111 or 800-627-6667. www.themirage.com.
Open May–Aug Mon–Fri 11am–7pm, weekends 10am–7pm. Rest of the year closes at
5:30pm. $12 (children under 10 free).*

Four connecting pools with a sand bottom and an artificial reef simulate the
natural environment for a group of dolphins here. You can tour the habitat,
which provides a sanctuary for Atlantic bottlenose dolphins and also serves
as a breeding facility, to watch trainers interact with these gentle mammals.

Feeding Frenzy at Atlantis Aquarium

*At The Forum Shops at Caesar's Palace, 3570 Las Vegas Blvd. S. 702-893-3807.
www.simon.com. Tours daily at 1:15pm & 5:15pm.*

More than 500 individual fish representing some 100 different species call this
50,000-gallon aquarium home. Make sure you drop by at 3:15pm or 7:15pm,
when you can watch divers enter the tank and feed the sharks, rays and other
denizens of the deep. The aquarium also offers a below-the-scenes tour of the
support facilities during the week. Dive shows and tours are free of charge.

If you're coming to Las Vegas and have a hankering to do some shopping, you'll be amazed at what's "in store" for you—namely everything from high-end designers (Chanel, Armani, Versace) to an assortment of novelty merchandise you can only imagine in your wildest dreams (think feline-shaped fabric footstools). Whether it be raindrops on roses or whiskers on kittens, you're guaranteed to find more than a few of your favorite things here.

The Forum Shops at Caesars Palace★★

At Caesars Palace, 3570 Las Vegas Blvd. S. 702-893-4800. www.simon.com.

It's been said that all roads lead to Rome, and if the foot traffic in The Forum Shops is any indication, that adage still rings true. With more than 100 stores, the 526,000sq ft mall known as the Forum Shops attracts as many as 200,000 visitors on a busy holiday weekend. No wonder it's billed as the most successful shopping center in the country in terms of sales volume per square foot.

The merchandise mix offers everything from high-fashion to novelty items. From DKNY to Escada to A/X Armani Exchange and from FAO Schwartz to Warner Brothers to Endangered Species, the Forum Shops is one of the wonders of Las Vegas. The Amen Wardy Home Store features an unusual selection of items for the home, and Estee Lauder allows customers to experiment on their own with a full line of make-up. Of course, FAO Schwartz is a blast for kids of all ages.

More Roads to Rome

Forum Shops is in the midst of another expansion, due for completion in the fall of 2004. The new three-level wing will extend from the existing retail, dining and entertainment venue to the Las Vegas Strip. An array of upscale specialty stores and restaurants will include Varvatos, Bruno Magli and Joe's Seafood, Prime Steak & Stone Crab (of South Beach, Miami fame).

- Don't leave the Forum Shops without trying one of Wolfgang Puck's restaurants: **Spago**, his signature property, or **Chinois**, his Asian-fusion delight. Have lunch at one and dinner at the other—just wait for the Forum sky to change from light to dark.

The Desert Passage★

Adjacent to (and connected to) the Aladdin, 3667 Las Vegas Blvd. S. 702-866-0703 or 888-800-8284. www.desertpassage.com.

Billed as "North America's first-ever shopping adventure," the Desert Passage is a 450,000sq ft shopping and entertainment complex where you'll feel as though you've just been transported to the great market cities of Tangier, Bombay and Marrakech.

From markets tucked into a towering mountainside to lively gathering places along a replica North African harborfront where thunderstorms are a regular occurrence, each element was carefully selected with help from architectural historians. Glazed mosaic tiles, storefronts made of sandstone blocks, Moorish archways and patterned iron grills bear testament to the degree of architectural detail here.

Shops and kiosks are grouped according to the area of the Desert Passage they are in, whether it be the Fragrance Market, Treasure House, the Lost City, Sultan's Palace, Sultan's Garden, Orangerie, Medina, the Dome of Spirits, the Hall of Lamps or Indian Gate. Each of the 140 dining and retail presentations reflects the Desert Passage intrigue from storefronts to merchandising. In a radical departure for Las Vegas, the complex offers direct access from the Las Vegas Strip.

If It's Moor You Want, It's Moor You'll Get

Some of the world-class retailers that are part of this shopping adventure are fashion retailers Cache, Betsey Johnson, Max Studio, and Herve Leger; the Hawaiian store Hilo Hattie; and the fine art and jewelry of Wyland Galleries and La Reverie. There is also an Endangered Species store, which is dedicated to raising public awareness of the plight of endangered species worldwide while providing a unique shopping experience.

Restaurants here include Commander's Palace, Prana Supper Club, Lombardi's Romagnia Mia, and Cheeseburger at the Oasis.

Fashion Show Mall

3200 Las Vegas Blvd. S., at the intersection of Las Vegas Blvd. & Spring Mountain Rd., across from Treasure Island. 702-369-8382. www.rouse.com.

Whoever said that "bigger is better" must have seen the new Fashion Show Mall. The first mall to open on the Strip, the venue holds the distinction of being not only its largest shopping establishment but, thanks to a recent expansion, also one of the largest shopping centers in the nation. In November 2002, the premier retail venue debuted Phase 1 of its four-year, $1 billion redevelopment plan, which will more than double the size of the center to over 1.9 million square feet.

Sundries in the Mall

Omni Chemists is a great place to stop if you're looking for sundry items that run the gamut from the unusual to the unheard-of . If you've been looking for Monkey Brand Tooth Powder from India, look no more. You've found it . . . along with myriad cosmetics, vitamins and other obscure and unique imported items, including great suntan products.

The renovation includes expanded flagship department stores from Neiman Marcus, Macy's and Robinsons-May, along with new stores for Saks Fifth Avenue, Dillard's, a prototype Bloomingdale's Home and the first Nordstrom in Nevada. When the expansion is completed in 2004 and Lord & Taylor opens, the center will be anchored by eight major department stores.

The completed expansion will welcome new retail, dining and entertainment experiences as well. Among them is the new east entrance featuring a 480ft "cloud" structure above a 72,000sq ft plaza on the Strip, which will present multimedia fashion images and live fashion shows. There will also be a food court with seating for 1,500 people.

Some of the newer stores include Futuretronics (electronics); Bag 'N Baggage (luggage); Honolulu Surf Co.(men's apparel and sporting goods); Aqua Beachwear; Adrienne Vittadini; Lunettes (eyewear); and Z Gallerie, with art, furniture and accessories for the home.

If you're hungry, snag a snack at the California Pizza Kitchen, the Café at Nordstrom or Mariposa at Neiman Marcus.

Grand Canal Shoppes

At The Venetian, 3355 Las Vegas Blvd. S. 702-414-1000 or 877-283-5423.
www.venetian.com.

Pigeons are all that's needed to make this Venice shopping experience feel any more real (the birds are there, but luckily they're outside the hotel). Strolling down the cobblestone walkways of this 500,000sq ft indoor mall at the Venetian, along nearly a quarter-mile of Venice's famed Grand Canal, you'll encounter more than 70 stores and boutiques. Many of The Grand Canal Shoppes have premiered here for the first time in the US market.

At St. Mark's Square (where the pigeons are found in the real Venice), you can take a 15-minute gondola ride down the 1,200ft-long **Grand Canal**[*] and be serenaded by a singing gondolier. Even if you skip the gondola ride, know that the shopping is a trip in itself. Be sure to visit Il Prato, which carries collectible masks and fine paper goods (including colorful glass-point fountain pens), and Ripa de Monti, which offers Venetian glass and collectibles. Another must-see store is Sephora, a 10,000sq ft beauty emporium dedicated to women's perfumes and cosmetics. Lladro, Tolstoys and Ancient Creations are also fun to browse for gifts.

Wonderful cafes and restaurants, many of them with canalside seating, are located in this retail area. Fashion concierges provide personalized fashion and shopping advice to international guests (who don't speak English), by appointment.

> ### Choo!
> Malaysian-born Choo was Princess Diana's preferred shoemaker, thanks to his handmade strappy sandals. When she needed shoes to match a particular outfit, Di would call Choo at his office and he would drive to Kensington Palace. Surrounded by samples of shapes, colors and fabrics, they would sit together on the floor to make final footwear choices.

Le Boulevard

At Paris Las Vegas, 3655 Las Vegas Blvd. S. 702-946-7000 or 800-634-3434.
www.parislv.com.

Le Boulevard cries out from every storefront, *Vive la différence!* The distinct French flavor is immediately apparent when you enter this 31,000sq ft retail space that connects Paris and its sister resort, Bally's, beginning at one casino and ending at the other. This French connection is called Le Boulevard and consists of authentic French boutiques in a chic Parisian setting.

Walk through the archway to Paris, where you will be greeted by the sight of cobblestone streets, winding alleyways and Parisian street lamps. One of the highlights is Napoleon's, a club featuring live entertainment, a cigar lounge and a walk-in humidor.

Some of the shops you won't want to miss include Les Memoires, a bed and bath shop offering everything from bath soaps to candles; and Les Elements, a garden shop with fresh and dried flowers, live and artificial topiaries, architectural statues, pottery and fine French linens.

La Cave offers private label and premium French wines and gourmet foods and cheeses. **Lenôtre**, named for culinary master Gaston Lenôtre, features fresh-baked croissants, breads and pastries as well as chocolates and fruit preserves. Then there is Le Journal, a 24-hour hotel gift shop, and Presse, a reproduction of a French magazine kiosk that sells newspapers, magazines and books.

A children's store, Les Enfants, offers French toys and games and also carries a line of children's apparel. Be sure to check out Judith Jack, a boutique that boasts one of the most extensive collections of designer Jack's sterling silver and marcasite jewelry, handbags and watches.

Making Scents

La Vogue is a boutique that features handbags, trendy jewelry and French perfumes, including Paris Las Vegas' own signature fragrance, C'est Si Bon. You can also buy this fragrance in La Menagerie de Paris, which carries fashionable Paris Las Vegas logo merchandise.

Via Bellagio

*At Bellagio, 3600 Las Vegas Blvd. S. 702-693-7111 or 888-987-6667.
www.bellagioresort.com.*

Fred Leighton

Not sure which necklace to wear with that sequined evening gown? Better stop in at Fred Leighton, which boasts the largest and most prestigious collection of estate and antique jewelry available to the public. You'll often find Fred himself at the store, telling the story behind each piece of jewelry. He also carries a rare collection of diamonds, rubies, emeralds and sapphires, including items from the collection of the Duchess of Windsor, as well as works from the Art Deco period and the magnificent jewels of Cartier, Van Cleef & Arpels, Mauboussin, Boucheron and Belperron.

Prada, Chanel and the fashion designs of Lagerfeld, Georgio Armani and Hermes always go into freestanding stores. Now, for the first time ever thanks to Bellagio, you can find them all under the same roof. Realizing the popularity of shopping in Las Vegas, Bellagio's retail area, Via Bellagio, has strived to bring together, for the first time anywhere, some of the world's greatest designers in one location.

Via Bellagio's inviting collection of upscale boutiques and shops combines the timeless with the avant-garde, the simple with the extravagant. Full collections from the designers mentioned above, as well as from Moschino, Gucci, Yves St. Laurent, and Tiffany & Co. are here for the taking. Besides high fashion, you'll find elegant jewelry, watches and gifts.

The Chanel Fashion Boutique offers the complete range of Chanel products: the Chanel Ready-to-Wear Collection designed by Karl Lagerfeld, handbags, accessories, shoes and Chanel fragrances. The Fine Jewelry Boutique offers the complete collection of Chanel jewelry.

Georgio Armani offers his Borgonuovo collections for men and women, including tailored clothing, dresses, sportswear, evening wear, cosmetics and accessories.

Prada offers ready-to-wear accessories and footwear as well as a new line of sports clothes. Gucci offers its trademark handbags, luggage and leather goods.

I t's touch and glow at Las Vegas resorts these days when it comes to the extravagant spas that each major property houses. From massage to body wraps and body-cleansing to relaxation techniques, you'll definitely get the royal treatment.

Canyon Ranch at the Venetian

3355 Las Vegas Blvd. S. 702-414-3600 or 877-220-2688. www.canyonranch.com.

Meanwhile, back at the Ranch, Canyon Ranch at the Venetian to be precise, the well-known name in health resorts is welcoming people to the first Spa-Club in Las Vegas. This peaceful and plush facility offers more than 120 spa services. It also features a fitness facility with a wellness center staffed by physicians and nutritionists. Canyon Ranch Salon *(4th floor)* offers a full list of beauty services from haircuts to makeovers.

Royal King's Bath

This 80-minute signature treatment, created for Canyon Ranch, includes:

- A dry brush exfoliation
- A soak in the bronze King's Bath, amidst aromatic essential oils and flower petals
- A relaxing massage at the treatment's end

Elemis Spa at the Aladdin

3667 Las Vegas Blvd. S. 866-935-3647 or 702-785-5SPA. www.aladdincasino.com or www.elemis.com/usa.

You'll revel in the exotic, earthy way of North African life at this oasis for the mind, body and spirit. Every bit of stress will melt away in the echo of Moroccan music, the flavors of herbal teas and treatments that incorporate rituals from 10 ancient cultures.

Some of the more popular among the 24 groundbreaking therapies include the Ceremony of Love with Hawaiian Wave Four Hand Massage, Marrakech Ceremony of the Sun, Jasmine Lulur Ritual, and the Exotic Frangipani Body Nourish Wrap.

Oasis Spa at Luxor

3900 Las Vegas Blvd. S. 702-730-5720 or 800-288-1000. www.luxor.com. Open 24 hours (except Tue). Patrons must be at least 18.

The Oasis Spa at the Egyptian-themed Luxor hotel is a place where healing hands, soothing waters and natural potions combine to create an exhilarating garden of sensory delights. An extensive menu of body wraps and scrubs, massage, facials, hyrotherapy, aromatherapy, body composition analysis, personal training and tanning is available. And each shower is individually appointed with its own scent of botanical bath and shower gels, shampoos, and conditioners.

Paris Spa by Mandara

At Paris Las Vegas, 3655 Las Vegas Blvd. S. 702-946-4366. www.mandaraspa.com. Advance reservations are recommended.

A Parisian-style hotel and a Balinese-inspired spa company may seem like an unlikely marriage but, at Paris Las Vegas, this couple has turned out to be a match made in pampering heaven. The name "Mandara" comes from an ancient Sanskrit legend about the gods' quest to find the elixir of eternal youth. The spa opened in Bali in 1996 with the concept it still adheres to today: to capture the Balinese way of giving from the heart.

Paris Spa, which uses Elemis natural aromatherapy products created in London, echoes the hotel's French theme with 24 treatment rooms adorned with embroidered silks, rich carpets and fine artwork. Custom-built private Spa Grande Suites boast oversize whirlpool baths, double-headed showers and a private lounge.

Rio Spa and Salon

3700 W. Flamingo Rd. 702-777-7779 or 800-777-7777. www.playrio.com.

Michael's Salon

Michael's specializes in hair sculpting, repairing, and color. They also offer manicures, pedicures, waxing and makeup application.

Blame it on Rio because after your visit you'll feel so relaxed from head to toe that you'll feel a glow for hours. Facials are a highlight here. The menu includes a contouring facial, for unsurpassed firming and toning, and a hydroxy acid facial—a five-part hydroxy acid skin-exfoliant system that gently smoothes the skin, removes surface debris, and stimulates cell renewal. There's even a deep cleansing and exfoliating facial for men and one for those hard-to-reach places on the back.

The Spa at Four Seasons

3960 Las Vegas Blvd. S. 702-632-5000 or 877-632-5000. www.fourseasons.com. Open to non-hotel guests Mon–Thu.

A spa for all seasons, this clubby facility has as its symbol Kuan Yin, the goddess of compassion, to convey how guests will be treated. The 12,000sq ft spa features 16 elegantly appointed treatment rooms, a Hydrotone Thermal Capsule, a relaxation room, and a eucalyptus steam room. You'll be pampered with traditional Balinese rituals, JAMU products made in Bali, and therapeutic services tailored to your specific needs. The signature treatment here includes a body scrub, body wrap, massage, reflexology and aromatherapy.

Must Be Seen: Nightlife

Las Vegas has always been at the forefront when it comes to gaming, hospitality and entertainment. But these days, the city even likes to lead when it dances. Recent steps have ensured some of the most exciting dance clubs and nightlife options anywhere. *Cover charges apply at most clubs (fees vary depending on night of the week).*

Cleopatra's Barge

At Caesars Palace, 3570 Las Vegas Blvd. S. 702-731-7110 or 800-634-6001. www.caesars.com. No cover or drink minimum.

Seated in 5ft of water, the popular 200-seat Cleopatra's Barge replicates the graceful craft that transported the royalty of Egypt on the Nile River during the days of Julius Caesar. Some of those details include a bowsprit hand-carved with the image of an Egyptian princess, furled sails hanging from the main mast, and statues of ancient pharaohs. Each night, a mysterious fog rolls in while an intricate rocking mechanism gives you the relaxing sensation of sailing the Nile. Meanwhile, cocktail waitresses dressed as Cleopatra's handmaidens carry beverages across a gangplank to a deck where you can relax in tiered seating that overlooks the barge. On the main deck is a dance floor bathed in multicolored computerized lights, where you can cut a rug every night.

Club Rio

At the Rio, 3700 W. Flamingo Rd. 702-252-7777 or 800-752-9746. www.playrio.com.

Club Rio at the Rio All-Suite Resort and Casino is the "granddaddy" of the Las Vegas nightlife scene. It was the very first club in the city in 1994, and the year after it opened, it was named one of the Top 10 Clubs in the country by *Rolling Stone* magazine. Its new tag is "no inhibition, all exhibition." Indeed, the night has a thousand eyes here, as huge video walls enable guests to watch themselves dance. Add to that a state-of-the-art laser system that showers the dance floor with flashing lights pulsating to the beat of the music, free shots of liquor, and all sorts of fun contests with cash prizes.

Bikinis

Life is a beach at the Rio, thanks to its newest hot spot, **Bikinis Beach and Dance Club**. This venue makes sure that its servers, bartenders, dancers and lifeguards are cool in more ways than one—they're all dressed in bikinis and swim trunks.

Curve

At the Aladdin, 3667 Las Vegas Blvd. S. 702-785-5525 or 877-333-WISH.
www.aladdincasino.com. Patrons must be 21.

One step inside the Aladdin's upscale nightspot and it's immediately apparent that Curve is a Las Vegas nightclub with a different bent. Billed as "a night in a millionaire's living room," Curve offers fun in every nook and cranny—the very configurations that give the club its name—along with the curved bar that holds court in one of the club's five elegant rooms. The place where the beautiful people now gather, the open-to-everyone $15 million hyper-lounge tips the ante with a new twist on late-night activity. The Aladdin calls it "nightlife evolved."

Curve itself evolved from a mix of lounges and mainstream nightclubs. Located in the back of the hotel's high-end gaming area, the London Club, Curve has a European ambience and it's a place where you can actually have a conversation.

Curve has a reputation for attracting celebrities (think Nicolas Cage, Dennis Quaid, Denzel Washington, Shaquille O'Neal)—sort of like taking the VIP areas of all the other clubs and rolling them into one.

Rooms to Choose

The largest of the five distinct rooms housed in Curve is known as the **Fountain Room**, for the fountain that forms its centerpiece. This is Curve's high-end lounge, complete with plush leather couches, a purple-felt pool table, and private booths with gold drapes.

Other choices include the Mega VIP Room, The Circle Room, The Curve Bar and another small VIP Room. A dress code is enforced and no food is served at Curve (except for star-studded special events, some of which are open to the public).

Ghost Bar

At the Palms Casino Resort, 4321 W. Flamingo Rd. 702-942-7777 or 866-725-6773. www.palms.com.

Billing itself as "the ultimate apparition," the Ghost Bar at the Palms is a sultry and sophisticated indoor-outdoor lounge and skydeck on the 55th floor of the hotel with a spectacular 360-degree view of Las Vegas.

You may have a close encounter of the celebrity kind here. The long list of notables that have visited the Ghost Bar includes the likes of Heather Locklear, Carmen Electra, Don Johnson and Nicolas Cage. If celebrity sightings aren't exciting enough for you, try the glass inset in the floor of the skydeck, which offers a jaw-dropping, straight-down view.

I'll Have One of Those

The Ghost Bar's signature **Ghostini** cocktail is a blend of Absolut vodka, Midori and sour mix.

The 8,000sq ft venue has a 30ft ghost-shaped soffit in the ceiling, which changes colors as a DJ spins an eclectic music mix. Floor-to-ceiling windows and custom, ultra-contemporary lounge furniture decorate the room. You can seek privacy in the intimate seating arrangements or mingle at the white terrazzo bar.

Rain In the Desert

At the Palms Casino Resort, 4321 W. Flamingo Rd. 702-942-7777 or 866-725-6773. www.palms.com.

If you want to see Rain in the Desert, you're going to have to go to the Palms. In fact, for a real rainwater experience, try one of the venue's eight water booths, patent leather banquettes filled with water.

From the moment you enter through the gold-mirrored mosaic tunnel, which is filled with changing light, fog and sound, you know you're in for a downpour of special effects. Inside, a water wall, a rain curtain, fog, haze and pyrotechnics such as 16ft fire plumes add to the atmosphere. The ultimate contemporary nightclub and concert venue, Rain combines performances by international headliners with an electrifying dance club, a private-event facility and intimate enclaves in one dynamic multisensory experience.

Luxury, private and VIP accommodations include a cabana level with private cabanas seating 8 to 12 guests. Each cabana includes a liquid-crystal display screen, lights that change colors, a mini-bar and specialty furniture. High above the cabanas, six lavish skyboxes boast private balconies overlooking the nightclub below. Food is available in all seating areas throughout the club courtesy of **The Grill**, Rain's private kitchen.

Risqué

At Paris Las Vegas, 3655 Las Vegas Blvd. S. 702-946-4589. www.parislv.com.

This ultra-lounge features a dessert bar with one-of-a-kind creations, prepared by renowned pastry chef Jean-Claude Canestrier. Here tropical fruit tempura and orange blossom crème brulée share the menu with soufflés and flambés, distinctive coffee drinks, premium cocktails, a wide selection of sakes, and a carefully chosen wine list.

From the sweet confections to the plush over-stuffed couches on balconies overlooking the Las Vegas Strip, this club seeks to create the ultimate "nightculture." Geared towards a sophisticated crowd, this ultra-lounge seeks out the chic in terms of its music, service and décor.

Risqué has a raised, lighted dance floor, a stylish Salon Privée with a private bar, a dessert bar nestled alongside the intimate dance floor, and a select late-night menu in Ah Sin downstairs *(see sidebar)*.

French velvet drapes, crystal chandeliers and mirrored lighting effects enhance the atmosphere at Risqué. Couches and ottomans can be moved to create intimate seating groups. Even the restrooms at Risqué are remarkable—a translucent wall separates the men's and women's restrooms which feature iridescent tile.

> **Food For Thought**
> Those enjoying the pleasures of Risqué have easy access to the cuisine of **Ah Sin,** located a level below and accessed by a winding staircase. Watch chefs in the open kitchen prepare delicacies from continental China and the island nations of the South Pacific, peppered with French accents that pay tribute to the two rich cultures. A sushi bar, an Asian grill, dim sum and a satay bar round out the offerings.

Shadow Bar

At Caesars Palace, 3570 Las Vegas Blvd. S. 702-731-7110 or 800-634-6661. www.parkplace.com/caesars. No cover or drink minimum. Patrons must be 21.

As you relax and enjoy a drink or a cigar at Shadow Bar, two female dancers undulate to music behind separate sheer scrims behind the bar. The dancers

appear as silhouettes, the effect created by a light that shines behind them. Caesars wanted women to be comfortable here, which is why the provocative dancers fade into the shadows. In between the 30-minute dance sets, flair bartenders exhibit their art, twirling and juggling bottles, pouring drinks over their shoulders, and scooping cherries out of the air.

Studio 54

At the MGM Grand, 3799 Las Vegas Blvd. S. 702-891-7254 or 800-929-1111. www.mgmgrand.com.

A high-energy trend-setting nightclub, Studio 54, named for the late, great New York City venue, claims to feature the most eclectic music mix in the country combined with state-of-the-art sound, lighting and staging. Music, courtesy of a DJ, ranges from cutting-edge sounds to the songs of the 1970s that made the original Studio 54 the epicenter of pop culture and style. The 22,000sq ft nightclub offers four dance floors and bars, an exclusive area on the second floor for invited guests, and several semi-private lounges capable of accommodating up to 400 people. If you're lucky, you might see one of the surprise acts (which in the past have included the Go-Gos and Prince) that take the stage on any given evening.

Tabu

At the MGM Grand, 3799 Las Vegas Blvd. S. 702-891-7254 or 800-929-1111. www.mgmgrand.com. Ladies get in free.

Symbolizing everything chic, cosmopolitan and innovative, Tabu's design is a distinct combination of modern fashion and refined style. A comfortable level of vocals allows guests to carry on conversations while taking in the scene and enjoying a cocktail. Although there's no dance floor, guests have been known to boogie on the 700-pound concrete tables—which house projected imagery systems that react to motion. Even laying a glass down on the table will cause the image on the table to change.

You won't want to miss the boat when it comes to two of the Las Vegas area's most popular day trips, Lake Mead and Hoover Dam. But if you're willing to venture a bit farther afield, the natural wonders of the Grand Canyon, the Mojave Desert and the Red Rock Country of Sedona, Arizona are all accessible within a day's drive of Las Vegas.

Hoover Dam★★★

31mi southeast of Las Vegas via US-93 South. 702-294-3523. www.hooverdam.com. Open year-round daily 9am–5pm. Closed Thanksgiving & Dec 25. $10.

Stretched like a gargantuan wall across the 800ft-deep Black Canyon of the Colorado River, Hoover Dam supplies water for more than 25 million people. It was built to control devastating floods on the lower Colorado River, and to provide water for drinking and irrigation.

Hoover Dam straddles the Nevada-Arizona border; tall clocks on each side of the line tell you the current time in both states. (Arizona doesn't change to Daylight Savings Time.) Called Boulder Dam until it was officially named for President Herbert Hoover in 1947, the site is the most popular reclamation project in the US. The phenomenal growth of Las Vegas has been attributed to the building of the dam and the thousands of people who moved here to construct it. Completed in February 1935, two years ahead of schedule, Hoover Dam was later cited by the American Society of Civil Engineers as one of America's seven modern civil-engineering wonders.

A Tour de Force

Guided tours leave every few minutes from the exhibition center at the top of the dam. Choose from the short sightseeing tours or the more comprehensive **Hard Hat Tour★★★** *(reservations: 702-294-3524).*

The Dam Facts

• More than 16,400 people toiled day and night for four years to build the dam.

• The dam is 660ft wide at its base with two spillways 50ft in diameter—each can handle the equivalent of Niagara Falls.

• Hoover Dam's 17 massive generators produce 4 billion kilowatt hours per year. That's enough to supply power for 1.3 million people.

Grand Canyon National Park ★★★

South rim is 260mi east of Las Vegas in Arizona. The north rim is 275mi east of Las Vegas. 520-638-7888. www.nps.gov/grca. Open year-round daily 8am. Closing hours vary. $10 for a 7-day pass.
The two main access points, the South Rim and the North Rim, are 214mi apart by road. Most visitor activities in the park are located on the South Rim. To reach the South Rim, take US-93 South through Boulder City to Kingman, AZ, about 90mi; exit on Hwy. 40 east to Williams, and drive north on Hwys. 64 & 180 to Grand Canyon Village. To get to the North Rim, take I-15 North to Hwy. 9 South; turn south on Hwy. 89 at the Mt. Carmel junction.

One look at the magnificent yawning crevice that ranks as one of the great natural wonders of the world and you'll realize that the Grand Canyon is everything it's cracked up to be—and more. Located in northwestern Arizona, this 1,904sq mi national park is now a World Heritage Site. The canyon was carved over the eons by the Colorado River, and today a giant swath of the earth's geological history appears in the colorful striated layers of rock that reach down more than a mile below the canyon's rim. At dawn and dusk, when the low-angle sun lights the vividly colored canyon walls, the 277mi-long Grand Canyon is an awesome and humbling sight.

SOUTH RIM ★★★

Grand Canyon Village – Site of the park headquarters, the main visitor center and the lion's share of hotels and restaurants and tourist facilities, this area includes the **Grand Canyon Village Historical District★**.

East Rim Drive★★★ – The 24mi road from Grand Canyon Village to the East Rim Entrance Station passes numerous dizzying viewpoints.

West Rim Drive★★ – Only free shuttle buses may travel this 8mi road from Grand Canyon Village, which stops at spectacular **viewpoints★★**.

NORTH RIM ★★

Open mid-May–mid-Oct, weather permitting. Less developed and more remote than the South Rim, the North Rim is also more spectacular, set in the deep forest of the Kaibab Plateau.

Bright Angel Point – From the visitor center adjacent to Grand Canyon Lodge, a paved .5mi trail ends at Bright Angel Point with glorious **views**★★★ of the canyon.

Cape Royal Road★ – This road extends 23mi from the Grand Canyon Lodge southeast across the Walhalla Plateau to Cape Royal. A spur route leads to Point Imperial, the highest spot on the canyon rim at 8,803ft.

No Yawns Here

A five-and-a-half-hour drive from Las Vegas, the canyon is best visited in April, May and September, when the summer crowds have left. The 7,000ft elevation keeps the South Rim from becoming unbearably hot in the summer; however the canyon bottom can reach temperatures of 110°F. From December to March, the upper canyon is usually snowbound. Plan on a two-night stay to see the South Rim and the scenic drives. If you have more time, you can take a mule trip *(reserve several months in advance)*, a helicopter tour or hike to the bottom of the canyon.

Death Valley National Park★★★

120mi west of Las Vegas via I-15 South and Hwy. 160. Go through Pahrump and take State Line Rd. to Death Valley Junction; at the junction, take Hwy. 190 to the park. Death Valley Visitor Center is located on Hwy. 190 at Furnace Creek. 760-786-3200. www.nps.gov/deva. Open year-round daily 8am–dusk. $5.

Although only one pioneer died trying to cross it, at first glance Death Valley seems to be appropriately named—when you stand in this vast, silent, stark landscape, it indeed seems inescapable. An enormous basin (130mi long and 5–25mi wide), the valley formed progressively as a block of the earth's crust sagged and sank between parallel mountain ranges, creating an astounding difference in elevation. Altitudes range from 282ft below sea level at Badwater to 11,049ft at Telescope Peak.

Designated as a national park under the 1994 Desert Protection Act, Death Valley is now the largest national park outside Alaska, covering more than 3.3 million acres. This is one of the hottest and driest places on earth: Annual precipitation averages less than two inches, and the highest temperature ever recorded in the US—134°F at Furnace Creek in 1913—has been exceeded only in the Sahara Desert.

Tips for Visiting

It's best to visit between late autumn and early spring, as the relentless summer sun heats the valley to some of the highest temperatures on earth. Be sure to check the gas and water in your car as well as the road conditions (check with the visitor center). Always carry plenty of drinking water and know the ins and outs of survival in the desert.

Best of Death Valley

Badwater Road★ – *Rte. 178, south of Furnace Creek*. This 36mi road follows Death Valley's descent to the lowest point in the Americas.

Zabriskie Point★★ – *Rte. 190, 4.5mi east of Furnace Creek*. This renowned point commands splendid views over Golden Canyon.

Dante's View★★★ – *24mi southeast of Furnace Creek via Rte. 190 to Dante's View Rd.* From a 5,475ft perch atop the Amargosa Range, this stunning **view**★★★ takes in the continent's most extreme elevation change.

Stovepipe Wells Sand Dunes★★ – *6mi east of Stovepipe Wells on Rte. 190.* The park's most accessible sand dunes pile up in billowing hills.

Scotty's Castle★ – *53mi north of Furnace Creek on Rte. 267.* This lavish Spanish-Moorish mansion, built in 1924 as a winter retreat for Chicago million-aire Albert Johnson, is named after Johnson's flamboyant friend, Walter Scott, aka "Death Valley Scotty."

Furnace Creek Inn & Resort

Hwy. 190 in Death Valley National Park. 760-786-2345. www.furnacecreekresort.com. 66 inn rooms; 224 ranch rooms. $240–$350, inn; $85–$159, ranch. There's no need to rough it in the desert when you can stay at the Furnace Creek Inn. The inn and adja-cent Furnace Creek Ranch have served as a welcoming oasis for visitors since the 1930s. You'll find everything you could ask for here—renovated air-conditioned rooms with ceiling fans, a restaurant, a spring-fed swimming pool, tennis courts, and an 18-hole golf course. The general store stocks camping supplies, but why would you want to leave this lovely place?

Lost City Museum of Archaeology★

63mi northeast of Las Vegas. 721 S. Moapa Valley Blvd., Overton, NV. Take I-15 North to Hwy. 169 and follow Hwy. 169 through Overton. The museum is about 15mi past Overton on the right. 702-397-2193. www.comnett.net-lostcity. Open year-round daily 8:30am–4:30pm. Closed Jan 1, Thanksgiving Day & Dec 25. $2.

The Lost City refers to the Pueblo Grande de Nevada, a series of Anasazi ruins set along the Muddy and Virgin river valleys in southern Nevada. The entire Anasazi culture, which established itself in the valley beginning about 300 BC, mysteriously disappeared from the area between AD 1150 and AD 1250.

At the height of their civilization in AD 800, the Anasazi inhabited the entire length of the valley along the banks of the Muddy River. What they left behind was pottery displaying a high degree of sophistication in ceramic art and design; chipped stone tools made from chert, a shiny glass-like stone; and thousands of petroglyphs (pictures etched in rock).

The museum was built on an Anasazi ruin to house artifacts that were being excavated from the Anasazi sites of Pueblo Grande before the newly dammed waters of Lake Mead covered them up forever. Today you can view those artifacts here, as well as the hilltop site where archaeologists have unearthed an actual **pueblo foundation**★.

Art of Pottery

When you look at the artifacts of the Anasazi, you'll see the distinctive geometric and highly stylized designs they used to decorate their pottery. These sophisticated people could create bowls and pots that were only 1/8-inch thick—without a pottery wheel. Archaeologists have been able to date the Anasazi site by the style of pottery they found there.

Sedona ★★

276mi southeast of Las Vegas in Arizona. Take US-93 South to I-40 East to US-89A South. Visitor Information: 928-282-7722 or www.sedonachamber.com.

This small city in northern Arizona owes its beauty and mystique to the variety of striking red buttes and spires that surround it. Sedona's red rocks have been a beacon for those seeking spiritual enlightenment since the 1980s, when some of its sites (Cathedral Rock, Bell Rock, Boynton Canyon) were found to emit concentrated electromagnetic energy.

Located in the heart of Arizona's **Red Rock Country** ★★★, Sedona is bounded by Oak Creek and Sycamore canyons, the Mogollon Rim and Verde Valley. The region takes its name from the rust color exposed in three mid-level strata of the Supai Group, the Hermit Formation and the Schnebly Hill Formation, all sculpted of sandstone between 270-300 million years ago.

Sedona's commercial area, north of the "Y" intersection of US-89A, teems with Native American crafts and New Age items. When the town gets too touristy, you're just a short drive—by off-road vehicle—away from Red Rock Country. Several companies offer off-road jeep tours, but if you're driving yourself, **Schnebly Hill Road** provides the most convenient backcountry access. The 12mi route turns from pavement to rutted dirt after the first mile, but if you press onward, you'll be rewarded by dazzling views of red rock formations and a panorama of the valley below.

Rooms With A View

Tuzigoot National Monument ★ – *23mi southwest of Sedona; off Rte. 279 in Clarksville, AZ. 928-634-5564. www.nps.gov/tuzi. Open year-round daily 8am–5pm (until 7pm in summer). Closed Dec 25.* This ancient Sinagua pueblo rises 120ft above the Verde River. At its height in the late 1300s, the site was home to about 225 people who lived in 86 ground-floor rooms and farmed the fertile valley.

Montezuma Castle National Monument ★ – *5mi south of Sedona in Camp Verde. Take I-17 South to Exit 289 and follow signs. 928-567-3322. www.nps.gov/moca. Open year-round daily 8am–5pm (until 7pm in summer).* Impossibly tucked into a natural limestone alcove 50–100ft above the floor of Beaver Creek, Montezuma Castle was part of a 12C Sinaguan community.

Lake Mead National Recreation Area★

27mi south of Las Vegas via US-93 at the junction of Lakeshore Scenic Dr. (Rte. 166). 702-293-8990. www.nps.gov/lame. Visitor center open year-round daily 8:30am–4:30pm. $3.

Smooth Sailing

Visit the **Alan Bible Visitor Center** *(Lakeshore Scenic Dr. at Rte. 93; 702-293-8990)*, a few miles west of Hoover Dam to pick up a useful map and information about recreational activities at the lake. Be sure to take a jaunt around the lake on the *Desert Princess*, a 100ft-long triple-deck paddleboat *(cruises depart from Lake Mead Marina near Boulder Beach)*.

Embracing two vast reservoirs on the Colorado River, this 2,350sq mi desert preserve was created in 1936 when the natural flow of the Colorado River was blocked by Hoover Dam. The largest manmade lake in the US, Lake Mead can hold enough water to cover the entire state of Nevada with six inches of water. More than nine million visitors each year come here to boat, fish, water ski, swim, camp, picnic and explore.

Lake Mead is the centerpiece of the Lake Mead Recreation Area, which also includes Lake Mojave to the south and the surrounding desert east to the edge of Grand Canyon National Park and north to Overton. The best way to see the blue lake, surrounded by barren mountains, canyon tops and plateaus, is, of course, by boat. There are numerous sandy beaches, secluded coves and narrow canyons that are only accessible by water. With water temperatures averaging 78 degrees in spring, summer and autumn, the clear lake is ideal for swimming.

Lake Mead Marina is the closest of the lake's five marinas to Las Vegas. Like the others, it has a general store (buy popcorn to feed the hundreds of carp that come up to the dock here—bring your camera, it's quite a sight!) and a restaurant where you can dine outside at the water's edge.

Las Vegas Hotels

The properties listed below were selected for their ambience, location and/ or value for money. Prices reflect the average cost for a standard double room for two people (not including applicable taxes, including the city's 7.25% hotel tax). Hotels in Las Vegas constantly offer special discount rates. Properties are located in Las Vegas, unless otherwise specified. For a listing of additional casino hotels, see Casinos. For a complete listing of hotels mentioned in this guide, see Index.

$$$$$	over $300	$$	$75–$125
$$$$	$200–$300	$	less than $75
$$$	$125–$200		

Luxury

Four Seasons Hotel $$$$ 424 rooms

3960 Las Vegas Blvd. S. 702-632-5000 or 877-632-5000. www.fourseasons.com.

A quiet respite in the city of excess, this elegant non-gaming property maintains its own distinctive identity even though its rooms occupy the 36th to

> **The Wild Range . . .**
> . . . of room rates, that is. Standard rates at the casino hotels range wildly from under $50 ("$39 summer special") to over $1,000 when big conventions come to town. So shop around before you book—with tens of thousands of rooms in town, you're bound to find a good deal.

39th floor of adjoining Mandalay Bay (accessible by private elevator). Spacious rooms are done in wood and rattan with floor-to-ceiling windows looking out on mountain and desert views. Guests have complimentary use of the health club and cabanas. For a memorable dining experience, try the artisan-aged beef at **Charlie Palmer Steak ($$$$)**.

Rio All-Suite Casino & Hotel $$$$ 2,500 rooms

3700 W. Flamingo Rd. 702-252-7777. www.playrio.com.

The Rio may be off the beaten track but it's hugely popular, drawing hip young party-goers from the Strip with its three nightclubs: Club Rio, the Voodoo Lounge, and Bikinis. Spacious well appointed suites feature floor-to-ceiling windows and a separate dressing area, plus a refrigerator and safe.

The Ritz-Carlton, Lake Las Vegas $$$$ 349 rooms
1610 Lake Las Vegas Pkwy., Henderson. 702-567-4700. www.ritz-carlton.com.

Nestled on the shores of the largest privately owned lake in the US, this golf and spa resort is quietly making waves. Evoking Mediterranean waterside villages with its clay-tile roofs and arched doorways, the Ritz wraps guests in luxury with marble baths and Frette linens. Treat yourself to a day at the Italian-inspired Spa Vita di Lago.

Moderate

Bally's Las Vegas $$$ 3,079 rooms
3645 Las Vegas Blvd. S. 702-967-4111 or 800-634-3434. www.ballyslv.com.

Bally's has maintained its quiet elegance and left the flash to other properties. Attractive standard rooms are among the largest in town at 500sq ft. Besides the casino, there's a swimming pool, a lovely spa, a salon and a shopping area. Bally's is also the home of Jubilee!, the second-longest running show in the city *(see Quintessential Vegas)*.

Emerald Suites $$$ 396 rooms
9145 Las Vegas Blvd. S. 702-948-9999 or 866-847-2002. www.emeraldsuites.com.

For an extended stay on the Las Vegas Strip in a non-gaming environment, Emerald Suites provides fully furnished one- and two-bedroom lodgings. Amenities include high-speed Internet access, and fully equipped kitchens. Relax in the pool here or spend a night on the town with free tickets to Las Vegas shows.

Flamingo Las Vegas $$$ 3,642 rooms
3555 Las Vegas Blvd. S. 702-733-3111 or 800-732-2111. www.flamingolasvegas.com.

Its name has survived from the 1940s era of Strip development, but the original Flamingo Hotel is no more. In 1993 the Hilton Corporation razed the Flamingo's original motel-style buildings, including the fortress-like "Bugsy's Suite" (named after the hotel's creator, "Bugsy" Siegel) with its false stairways and bulletproof office. The updated Flamingo includes six towers filled with contemporary guest rooms, swimming pools, a wedding chapel in a tropical setting, and a wildlife habitat.

Green Valley Ranch

$$$ 247 rooms

I-215 & Green Valley Pkwy.,
Henderson. 702-617-7777.
www.stationcasinos.com.

This suburban casino has a backyard that's one of the most happening places in town. With a spectacular view of the Las Vegas Strip, this eight-acre landscaped recreation area features infinity-edge pools, private cabanas and a sand beach. Spacious rooms are decorated in Old World style; many overlook the Strip. When you're not in your room, you can relax at the spa, listen to live entertainment, or dance the night away at the sleek Whiskey Bar, the area's hip new night spot.

Hard Rock Hotel

$$$ 657 rooms

4455 Paradise Rd. at Harmon Ave. 702-693-5000. www.hardrockhotel.com.

You know from the moment that you see the chandelier with 32 gold saxophones hanging from it that you're in the Hard Rock Hotel. Set off the Strip, this 11-story property features a casino decorated with memorabilia from past and present rock stars. The world's hottest music acts perform in the 1,200-seat theater, and Gen Xers flock to Baby's, the hotel's nightclub. Sleek rooms are done in a musical motif with leather headboards and French doors. Of course, there's a Hard Rock Café on the premises, and **Nobu ($$$)** serves the acclaimed Japanese cuisine of chef Nobu Matsuhisa.

Hyatt Regency Lake Las Vegas

$$$ 496 rooms

1600 Lake Las Vegas Pkwy., Henderson. 702-567-1234. www.lakelasvegas.hyatt.com.

The Hyatt Regency's location on Lake Las Vegas affords guests easy access to a host of water sports. Hand-painted armoires and Moroccan headboards highlight the airy rooms. Many who stay at this Moorish-style hotel would rather drive on the Jack Nicklaus-designed 18-hole golf course than drive into the city. The Hyatt's dining room, **Japanego ($$$$)**, is acclaimed for its sushi and Pacific Rim cuisine.

The Orleans

$$$ 1,426 rooms

4500 W. Tropicana Ave. at Arville St. 702-365-7111. www.orleanscasino.com.

With its French Quarter theme and Mardi Gras ambience, the Orleans offers well-appointed oversized rooms that the hotel calls "petite suites." A 9,000-seat arena hosting concerts and sporting events; 13 restaurants including **Canal Street ($$$)**, known for its steak and seafood; a spa; a 70-lane bowling alley; and a movie-theater complex assure that you'll never be bored. If this isn't enough action for you, take the free shuttle to the Strip.

Budget

Alexis Park Resort & Spa

$$ 500 suites

375 E. Harmon Ave. between Koval Lane & Paradise Rd. 702-796-3300. www.alexispark.com.

Set amid winding paths, waterfalls and lush greenery, this resort filled with two-story white stucco villas began life as a complex of town homes. Located a half-mile from the Strip, Alexis Park doesn't have a casino. What it does have are tennis courts, three pools and a spa. Tastefully decorated suites are equipped with refrigerators, mini-bars and VCRs; larger units have vaulted ceilings, gas fireplaces and whirlpool tubs.

Circus Circus $$ 4,000 rooms
2880 Las Vegas Blvd. S. 702-734-0410 or 800-634-3450. www.circuscircus.com.

Opened in 1968, Circus Circus was the city's first gaming establishment to offer fun for all ages. Today the casino occupies the main floor, while the second floor is a fantasyland of carnival games, state-of-the-art arcade games and a free circus arena in which acts perform. Guests can choose among accommodations in the Skyrise Tower, the three-story Manor motor lodge or the RV park. Of the resort's nine restaurants, **The Steakhouse ($$$)** is famed for its prime cuts of aged mesquite-grilled beef.

Echo Bay Resort & Marina $$ 50 rooms
On Lake Mead, in Overton. 702-394-4000 or 800-752-9669. www.echobay7c.com.

The whole family will have fun at this resort on the shores of Lake Mead—even Fido is welcome here. Using the comfortable hotel as a base, you can rent a houseboat, ski boat or other watercraft. The resort's adjacent RV park offers daily and monthly rates and a range of services including laundry, showers and a restaurant.

French Quarter Suites $$ 96 suites
4777 Cameron St. 702-365-5500 or 800-359-4827. www.frenchquarterresort.com.

Offering clean, affordable one- and two-room suites, this property is located adjacent to Orleans casino. All suites have a balcony or patio and come with a fully equipped kitchen, cable TV, and Internet access. If you get tired of all the action at the casino next door, you can always come back to the hotel and take a dip in the pool. Laundry facilities are also available on site.

Golden Nugget $$ 1,901 rooms
129 Fremont St. 702-385-7111 or 800-846-5336. www.goldennugget.com.

Las Vegas' first luxury hotel, the Golden Nugget may be downtown, but it still has its share of panache. Remodeled and reopened in 1987, its gold-and-white understated elegance stands out amidst the neighboring neon. Refurbished rooms are spacious and beautifully appointed with rich woods. On display in the lobby is the "Hand of Faith," the world's largest golden nugget, valued at $1 million.

Sunset Station $$ 457 rooms
1301 W. Sunset Rd. at Stephanie St., Henderson. 702-547-7777. www.sunsetstation.com.

This casino hotel located just minutes from Lake Mead and Hoover Dam brings a touch of the Mediterranean to the area with its Spanish-style architecture and colorful centerpiece Gaudi bar. In addition to its 3,000 slot and video-poker machines, Sunset Station books headliners at its 5,000-seat outdoor amphitheater. Dining options include several upscale restaurants as well as a food court.

Viva Las Vegas Villas $$ 32 rooms
1205 Las Vegas Blvd. S. 702-384-0771 or 800-574-4450. www.vivalasvegasvillas.com.

Tucked behind the Viva Las Vegas Wedding Chapel, the largest chapel on the strip, this bed-and-breakfast caters to the just-married with its individually themed rooms. Blue Hawaii takes its cue from the Elvis movie of the same name, with a beach mural and palm trees towering over the bed; the Intergalactic room features a transporterbay shower. In the Camelot room, you'll find a knight in shining armor.

Must Eat: Restaurants

The venues listed below were selected for their ambience, location and/or value for money. Rates indicate the average cost of an appetizer, an entrée and a dessert for one person (not including tax, gratuity or beverages). Most restaurants are open daily and accept major credit cards. Call for information regarding reservations, dress code and opening hours. Restaurants listed are located in Las Vegas unless otherwise noted. For a complete listing of restaurants mentioned in this guide, see Index.

| $$$$ | over $50 | $$ | $15–$30 |
| $$$ | $30–$50 | $ | under $15 |

Luxury

Emeril's New Orleans Fish House $$$$ Creole/Cajun
MGM Grand, 3799 Las Vegas Blvd. S. 702-891-7374. www.mgmgrand.com.

Celebrity chef Emeril Lagasse hits the Vegas strip with his signature "Bam!" You'll swear you're in New Orleans when you taste such kicked-up Creole delights as barbecue shrimp and andouille-crusted redfish. Wash down the spicy dishes with a selection from the award-winning wine list.

Michael's $$$$ Continental
The Barbary Coast, 3595 Las Vegas Blvd. S. Dinner only. 702-737-7111. www.barbarycoastcasino.com.

Named for Michael Gaughn, the owner of the hotel in which it resides, this restaurant has long had the reputation for being one of the best in Las Vegas. Michael's only seats 40, so reservations can be hard to get. Whole Maine lobster, veal chop Florentine and Chateaubriand (for two) never fail to disappoint. For dessert, bananas Foster and cherries jubilee are flamed at table.

Nobhill $$$$ Regional American
MGM Grand, 3799 Las Vegas Blvd. S. Dinner only. 702-891-7433. www.mgmgrand.com.

Inspired by the traditional neighborhood restaurants found throughout the San Francisco area, Chef Michael Mina has combined that city's most innovative dishes into a unique menu. The dining room centers on a wood-fired bread oven; signature dishes such as lobster pot pie and North Beach cioppino are complemented by organic vegetables and greens.

Picasso　　　　　　　　　　　　$$$$　Mediterranean
Bellagio, 3600 Las Vegas Blvd. S. Dinner only. 702-693-7111. www.bellagio.com.

With original Picasso paintings and ceramics adorning the restaurant and a décor valued at up to $60 million, Picasso gives a whole new meaning to the art of dining. James Beard award-winning chef Julian Serrano offers two different prix-fixe menus daily, a five-course tasting menu and a four-course à la carte menu highlighting the sunny flavors of southern France and Spain.

Moderate

Isis　　　　　　　　　　　　　　$$$　Continental
The Luxor, 3900 Las Vegas Blvd. S. Dinner only. 702-262-4773. www.luxor.com.

You have to take a private elevator to get to this second-floor feast for the senses inside the Luxor hotel. Once inside the circular room, you'll settle into upholstered demilune booths. Crisp sliced duck in cassis-and-ginger sauce, and lobster tail with seafood mousse in buttery puff pastry will delight the palate. Favorite desserts include baked Egypt, Luxor's take on baked Alaska.

Jazzed Café & Vinoteca　　　　　　$$$　Northern Italian
8615 W. Sahara Ave., at Durango Ave. (in Lakeside Plaza). Dinner only. 702-233-2859. www.jazzedcafe.com.

This brightly-colored hangout with live jazz every night is considered by many to be the best undiscovered restaurant in town. Don't leave without trying one of the café's signature made-to-order risottos. There are 17 different risottos on the menu at any given time, featuring such flavors as orange-and-anchovy, white truffle, and tomato-basil.

Mon Ami Gabi　　　　　　　　　　$$$　French
Paris Las Vegas, 3655 Las Vegas Blvd. S. 702-944-4224. www.parislv.com.

Named for chef Gambino Soletino, this restaurant offers a charming bistro décor that spells Paris all the way. Its patio dining on the Strip (complete with misters to cool patrons in summer) is one of the best people-watching sites in the city, and a great spot to view the Bellagio fountain show. At night, the setting turns romantic with candlelight and bistro classics such as steak frites.

Pamplemousse Restaurant · $$$ French

400 E. Sahara Ave., just east of Paradise Rd. 702-733-2066. www.pamplemousserestaurant.com.

One of Vegas' long-standing favorites, Pamplemousse ("grapefruit" in French) has been pleasing diners in the city for more than 23 years. You'll often spot celebrities eating in this romantic country-French setting with its private alcoves. There is no written menu; your waiter will rattle off the evening's selections—specialties include duck, veal and seafood.

Rosemary's · $$$ New American

West Sahara Promenade, 8125 W. Sahara Ave. 702-869-2251. www.rosemarysrestaurant.com.

Michael and Wendy Jordan are giving the celebrity chefs in Vegas a run for their money with a top-notch gastronomical experience. (That's not surprising, since Michael trained under acclaimed New Orleans chef Emeril Lagasse.) From Hawaiian Ahi tuna au poivre to herb-crusted veal tenderloin, everything on the menu is prepared with the utmost attention to detail. Rosie's Goodnight Kiss, an after-dinner coffee drink (Godiva chocolate liqueur, Frangelico and mocha cappuccino) is guaranteed to give you sweet dreams.

Terrazza · $$$ Italian

Caesars Palace, 3570 Las Vegas Blvd. S. 702-731-7568. www.parkplace.com/caesars/lasvegas.

Terrazza doesn't do Italian like the rest, you'll have to go somewhere else if you want that heavy tomato sauce. This restaurant focuses on the essences of Mediterranean cuisine—olive oil, capers, olives, rosemary, fennel and garlic. They're used with a light hand in entrées such as rigatoni alla Boscaiola, with peas, mushrooms and mascarpone cheese; and risotto with spring vegetables.

Budget

The Bootlegger Bistro · $$ Italian

7700 Las Vegas Blvd. S., between Warm Springs & Blue Diamond Rds. Open 24hrs. 702-736-4939. www.bootleggerlasvegas.com.

For those who want a touch of Las Vegas the way it used to be, the Bootlegger is for you. Owned by Maria and Albert Perri, and their daughter, Lorraine Hunt (lieutenant governor of Nevada), this restaurant offers real home-style Italian cooking (Mama Maria comes in three times a week to oversee the making of the sauces, meatballs and sausage) along with great old-fashioned Vegas entertainment. On Friday and Saturday nights, Hunt's husband, Blackie, and entertainer Sonny King (Jimmy Durante's partner for 30 years) do a show called Off The Cuff.

Center Stage
$$ American

Jackie Gaughan's Plaza Hotel and Casino, 1 Main St. Dinner only. 702-386-2110.
www.plazahotelcasino.com.

As you might guess from the restaurant's name, the view is the main attraction here. With its circular dining room and raised platform seating surrounded on three sides by windows, Center Stage is the perfect place to watch the Fremont Street Experience sound-and-light spectacular. Enjoy plentiful portions of orange roughy Française and roasted prime rib during the show.

Chin Chin
$$ Chinese

New York-New York, 3790 Las Vegas Blvd. S. 702-740-6300. www.newyorknewyorkcasino.com.

True to its name, which means "to your health," this California chain offers "lite" dishes—prepared with little or no oil—and uses no MSG in its food. You can watch chefs in the open exhibition kitchen whip up tasty dim sum appetizers, shredded chicken salad with red ginger dressing, and Anthony's Special Noodles (lo mein with chicken in a spicy cilantro sauce).

Gordon Biersch
$$ American

Hughes Center, 3987 Paradise Rd. at E. Flamingo Rd. 702-312-5247. www.gordonbiersch.com.

A San Francisco-based brew pub, Gordon Biersch is the place to drink in the singles scene—especially on weekends. The restaurant pairs a short list of well-made lagers (no ales) with a large eclectic menu. Many of the selections—fettuccine with grilled chicken, shrimp and andouille sausage; sweet and spicy cashew-chicken stir-fry—are highly seasoned, so drink up.

Cheeseburger at the Oasis
$ American

Desert Passage at the Aladdin, 3667 Las Vegas Blvd. S. 702-73' ,. www.aladdincasino.com.

Say "cheese." The fifth in a string of successful restaurants that began in Hawaii (Cheeseburger in Paradise), this eatery lists only one cheeseburger on its menu. But as far as other burgers go, they've got hamburgers, garden burgers, turkey burgers and lots more. You can add guacamole, mushrooms, and/ or bacon for an additional charge. Save room for the signature mud pie.

Tilted Kilt
$ Irish

The Rio, 3700 W. Flamingo Rd. 702-777-2463. www.playrio.com.

Decorated with a mix of Celtic artifacts and pop-culture memorabilia, the Tilted Kilt gives the Irish pub scene a whole new twist. Here you can play pool and darts, and taste any of 24 premium beers on tap. Waitresses clad in midriff tops and mini-kilts serve unorthodox pub fare such as drunken clams, steamed in the beer of your choice.

Must-Eat Buffets

When once is not enough, insofar as food servings are concerned, then a Las Vegas buffet is where you want to be. Here you can have a full plate every minute—breakfast, lunch and dinner. Once the home of the $1.99 buffet, Las Vegas has increased both the prices and the quality of the food in recent years. Some buffets, such as Paris and Bellagio, top $20 for dinner—double the price of most of the buffets in town—but the food is worth the price.

Bally's Big Kitchen Buffet is one where you can stick with traditional fare or go with fresh-cooked Chinese selections *(702-739-7111; www.ballyslv.com; $ breakfast & lunch, $$ dinner)*.

Bellagio serves venison, duck breast, steamed clams and king crab legs in addition to the usual buffet fare *(702-693-7111; www.bellagiolasvegas.com; $ breakfast; $$ lunch & dinner, $$$ dinner Fri–Sat)*.

Carnival World Buffet at the Rio features a moderately priced Mongolian grill where you can pick your own ingredients and have them cooked with chicken, beef or shrimp *(702-252-7777; www.playrio.com; $–$$)*.

Paris Las Vegas offers food stations from various French provinces, as well as an incredible assortment of French pastries and fresh crêpes cooked to order *(702-946-7000; www.parislv.com; $ breakfast, $$ lunch & dinner)*.

The Un-Buffet

Bally's Sterling Brunch is not a buffet in the traditional sense *(702-967-7999; www.ballyslv.com; $$$$)*. Voted the number-one Sunday brunch in Las Vegas, the Sterling Brunch takes place each Sunday in Bally's Steakhouse. The menu changes weekly, but you can always expect sturgeon caviar, Cordon Rouge champagne, fresh sushi, made-to-order omelets, oysters, beef tenderloin and lobster.

More Must-Eat Buffets

Aladdin's Spice Market Buffet, with its variety of international stations, was voted the city's "Best Buffet" in a 2003 readers' poll by the Las Vegas Review-Journal *(702-785-5555; www.aladdincasino.com; $ breakfast & lunch, $$ dinner; kids 4 and under eat free)*.

The Flamingo's Paradise Garden Buffet has a view of the Wildlife Habitat and a prime rib, shrimp and crab buffet every night *(702-733-3111; www.flamingolasvegas.com; $ breakfast & brunch, $$ dinner)*.

Main Street Station's Garden Court Buffet has great prices and terrific food *(702-387-1896; www.bodygaming.com; $ breakfast, lunch & dinner; kids under 3 eat free)*.

Pharoah's Pheast at the Luxor includes a 30ft salad bar and a homemade pizza station *(702-262-4000; www.luxor.com; $ breakfast & lunch, $$ dinner; half-price for children 3–11)*.

The following abbreviations may appear in this Index: NHS National Historic Site; NM National Monument; NMem National Memorial; NP National Park; NHP National Historical Park; NRA National Recreational Area; NWR National Wildlife Refuge; SP State Park; SHP State Historical Park; SHS State Historic Site.

Las Vegas Index

Las Vegas Index

Photos Courtesy Of:

Photo Credits continued from inside back cover.

Splendido & Chef David Lee (Toronto, ON): icon pp. 120-124; Dee Dee Couch: icon 90-93; Rosemary's: 122; John Connelly: 18, icon 80-85